MASTERS OF THE UNIVERSE: BIOGRAPHY OF THE NFL OWNERS AND HOW THEY GOT THERE

by Bishop Weaver

CONTENTS

Title   1
AFC East   5
New York Jets Owner Woody Johnson   6
Miami Dolphins Owner Stephen M. Ross   10
The Buffalo Bills Owner Terry Pegula   15
Patriots Owner Robert Kraft   21
Pittsburgh Steelers Owner Arthur Rooney II   26
Pittsburgh Steelers Owner Arthur Rooney II   27
Cleveland Browns Owner Jimmy Haslam   29
Cincinnati Bengals Owner Mike Brown   33
Baltimore Ravens Owner Steve Bisciotti   45
AFC South   48
Jacksonville Jaguars Owner Shahid Khan   49
Indianapolis Colts Owner Jim Irsay   52
Tennessee Titans Owner Amy Adams Strunk   55
Houston Texans Owners Bob and Janice McNair   57
AFC West   61
Denver Broncos CEO Joe Ellis (Running the Franchise for   62
Pat Bowlen)
Oakland Raiders Owner Mark Davis   67
Kansas City Chiefs Owner Clark Hunt   73
Los Angeles Chargers Owner Dean Spanos   77
NFC   80
NFC East   81
Cowboys Owner Jerry Jones   82
Redskins Owner Daniel Snyder   89
New York Giants Owners Jon Mara and Steve Tisch   96
Philadelphia Eagles Owner Jeffrey Lurie   99
NFC North   103

Chicago Bears Owner Virginia Halas McCaskey 104
Minnesota Vikings Owner Zygi Wilf 106
Detroit Lions Owner Martha Ford 109
The Green Bay Packers, owned by Green Bay Packers, Inc. 112
NFC South 117
New Orleans Saints Owner Gail Benson 118
Tampa Bay Buccaneers Owner Bryan Glazer 122
Carolina Panthers Owner David Tepper 124
Atlanta Falcons Owner Arthur Blank 130
NFC West 133
San Francisco 49ers Owner Jed York 134
The Los Angeles Rams Owner Stan Kroenke 137
Arizona Cardinals Owner Bill Bidwell 144
Seattle Seahawks Recently Passed Owner Paul Allen 147

AFC EAST

NEW YORK JETS OWNER WOODY JOHNSON

Robert Wood "Woody" Johnson IV (born April 12, 1947) is an American businessman, philanthropist and diplomat currently serving as United States Ambassador to the United Kingdom. He is the great-grandchild of Robert Wood Johnson I (co-founder of Johnson & Johnson). He is the owner of the National Football League's New York Jets with his brother, Christopher.

Johnson was born in New Brunswick, New Jersey, USA. He is Betty's son (Wold) and the four-year president of Johnson & Johnson, Robert Wood Johnson III. Johnson grew up in the affluent parts of northern New Jersey with four siblings, Keith Johnson, Billy Johnson, Elizabeth "Libet" Johnson, and Christopher Wold Johnson, attending Millbrook School. He graduated from Arizona University. Johnson then worked at Johnson & Johnson with menial summer jobs expected to rise to the top of the family business. In the 1980s, Johnson became involved in full-time charities. He is a Foreign Relations Council member. His family had both lupus and juvenile diabetes, motivating Johnson to play a role in raising funds to prevent, treat and cure autoimmune diseases. He led efforts to increase research funding for these diseases on Capitol Hill and at the National Institutes of Health and personally contributed to causes related to diabetes after his daughter, Casey, was diagnosed with the disease. After his daughter Jaime was found to have lupus, he started a research foundation, the Alliance for Lupus Research.

On January 18, 2000, Johnson bought the Jets for $635 million, the third highest price for a professional sports team and the highest price for one in New York. Johnson, who also owns the New York Knicks court seats, outbid the $612 million offered by Cablevision chairman Charles Dolan, who owns Madison Square Garden, the Knicks, and the Rangers. The team sold over $100 million higher than expected by some sports finance analysts. Forbes now values the team at $1.8 billion. Johnson announced plans after purchasing the Jets to move them to Manhattan's proposed West Side Stadium. However, after the defeat of the project in 2005, Johnson announced that the Jets would move as an equal partner with the Giants to a new Meadowlands Stadium. The new stadium began on April 10, 2010 with MetLife acquiring naming rights.

Johnson served on the search committee of the NFL Commissioner, where a list of 185 successor candidates for Paul Tagliabue was narrowed down to Roger Goodell as the final choice. Johnson is the Chairman and Chief Executive Officer of Johnson Company, Inc., a private investment firm founded in 1978. In August 2006, Johnson was asked to testify to his participation in a tax avoidance scheme before the Permanent Subcommittee on Investigations of the Senate. A report from the Senate said Johnson, along with others, was able to buy about $2 billion in capital losses for relatively small fees that they used to eliminate taxable gains from stock sales. As a result, the U.S. Treasury lost an estimated revenue of $300 million. Johnson said in a statement that his lawyers had advised him in 2000 that the transaction "was consistent with the Tax Code." After that view was challenged by the Internal Revenue Service in 2003, Johnson settled with the IRS in 2006 and agreed to pay 100% of the tax due plus interest.

Johnson was chairman of the pre-commissioning unit for the San Antonio-class ship USS New York City. He orchestrated a fundraiser in New York City in May 2008 that brought in $7 million for John McCain in one evening, by far the largest amount collected up to that point by a campaign struggling to raise money. Johnson also provided substantial funding for the Minneapolis–St 2008 Republican National Convention. A member of the St. Paul Convention host committee; Johnson contributed personally from a $10 million shortfall and requested friends to help cover the convention deficit. Woody Johnson announced in 2011 that he would endorse former Massachusetts Governor Mitt Romney for the 2012 U.S. Presidential election.On September 23, 2013, Johnson hosted a fundraiser at his home in New York City for the Republican National Committee.In June 2015, Johnson was appointed National Finance Chairman for the 2016 presidential campaign of Jeb Bush. In May 2016, Johnson endorsed Donald Trump as president. Later, President Trump made him the United States Ambassador to the United Kingdom. Vice-President Mike Pence swore him in at the Oval Office on August 21, 2017. On 8 November 2017, Johnson presented his credentials to Queen Elizabeth II, formally becoming

Ambassador.

In 1977, Johnson married Nancy Sale Johnson, the former fashion model. Before they divorced in 2001, they had three children. Daughter Casey Johnson died of diabetic ketoacidosis in early 2010. In 2009, Johnson married Suzanne Ircha Johnson, a former Sandler O'Neill & Partners equity managing director and former actress. They have two children. Johnson has homes in Bedminster Township, New Jersey, and Manhattan, New York City Johnson has two children.

The Jets Under Johnson

Since 2000, the New York Jets have been one of the most mediocre teams in the NFL, having their only highlights limited to the early 00's playoff runs with Chad Pennington at the Helm, and the brief Rex Ryan years in the late 00's with their apex being achieved during a 2010-2011 season Playoff Upset of the New England Patriots in the Divisional Round of the NFL Playoffs. Other than that, the New York Jets pale in comparison for success where compared to their stadium mates, the Giants.

MIAMI DOLPHINS OWNER STEPHEN M. ROSS

Stephen M. Ross is Occupation Chairman of The Related Companies, and 95 percent owner of Miami Dolphins. Ross is The Related Companies ' chairman and majority owner, a global real estate development firm he founded in 1972. The Time Warner Center, where Ross lives and works, as well as the Hudson Yards Redevelopment Project, is best known for his development. According to Forbes magazine, Ross had a net worth of $4.4 billion.

Ross is also the main owner of the Miami Dolphins and Hard Rock Stadium.Ross is a major benefactor of his alma mater, the University of Michigan; with a lifetime contribution of $378 million to the university, and he is the largest donor in university history. He attended Florida University and then moved to Michigan Business School University where he earned his B.S. degree in Accounting in 1962. He subsequently received a Juris Doctor from the 1965 Wayne State Law School and an LL.M. Degree in Taxation from the New York University School of Law in 1966.

These later degrees were financed by a loan from his

uncle, the businessman Max Fisher, whom Ross called "the most important role model and inspiration for me in life." Ross began his career as a tax attorney at Coopers & Lybrand in Detroit. He moved to New York City in 1968 and took up a position as assistant vice president in Laird Inc.'s real estate subsidiary and then worked in Bear Stearns ' corporate finance department. In 1972, he left his main employment and living off $10,000, he used his knowledge of federal tax law to organize deals for wealthy investors enabling them to shelter income with the generous incentives given by the federal government to promote the construction of affordable federally subsidized housing. He was very successful, earning $150,000 in his first year.

Using his earnings as well as his newfound experience, he began to develop real estate on his own and quickly gained a solid reputation in the American real estate arena with a focus on high-quality architecture and engineering. He has developed apartments, condominiums, retail, office parks and mixed-use developments with a focus on the northeastern United States and Florida. He founded The Related Companies, a property development company, in 1972.

The Related Companies Related is an integrated and diversified property development company. Development, acquisitions, management, finance, marketing and sales are part of its business. Related is headquartered in New York City, Boston, Chicago, Los Angeles, Las Vegas, San Francisco, South Florida, Abu Dhabi, and Shanghai and have offices and Real Estate Developments. The company directly employs approximately 2,000 people. The company's existing portfolio of real estate assets, valued at over $15 billion, is made up of mixed-use, residential, retail, office, trade show and affordable properties in what the company calls "premier high-barrier-to-entry markets."

In February 2008, Ross bought 50 percent of the Miami Dolphin franchise, Dolphin Stadium (now known as Hard Rock Stadium) and surrounding land from then-owner Wayne Huizenga for $550 million, with an agreement to later become the Dolphins' managing general partner. Ross closed the purchase of an additional 45 percent of Wayne Huizenga's team on January 20, 2009. The total value of the deal was $1.1 billion. This means that Ross is now the franchise and stadium owner of 95 percent of the team. Ross announced his intention to keep Bill Parcells as the director of football operations at the time. Later, shortly before the 2010 NFL season, Parcells stepped down from his position. Ross has been instrumental in bringing in Gloria Estefan, Marc Anthony, Venus Williams, and Serena Williams as the team's minority owners since buying the Dolphins.

In 2013, Ross pushed for multi-million-dollar public funding from the state of Florida and taxpayers from Miami-Dade to help restore Hard Rock Stadium, the home field of the Dolphins. After this effort failed in the Florida legislature, a team spokesman said that Ross had no intention of moving the team, but that the future of the Dolphins in the Miami area was bleak under an eventual future owner. Although Ross said he intended to keep the Dolphins "in town," speculation was raised that the team might seek to move out of Miami to a nearby location such as Palm Beach.

He is also a partner in RSE Ventures. RSE was co-founded in 2012 by Ross and Matt Higgins (businessman), former vice president of the New York Jets, and current Vice President of the Miami Dolphins. RSE establishes, owns and operates a variety of companies, including the Drone Racing League, Thuzio, VaynerMedia and Relevant. Ross and Carl Peterson own Kangaroo Media, producer of Relevant.

In 2004, by donating $100 million to the school, Ross made the largest single contribution (at the time) to the University of Michigan. The University renamed its business school, Ross Business School in his honor. Ross was announced on September 12, 2013 to commit an additional $200 million gift to the University to be distributed equally between the Ross School of Business and the athletic department of the University. It replaced the 2013 contribution of $115 million from Charlie Munger as the largest single gift in the history of the University. Ross donated an additional 50 million on September 20, 2017 to the University of Michigan, most of which would support student career development programs, innovative action-based learning experiences, and resources to attract and develop junior faculty. He was on the NYC 2012 Executive Committee, New York's initiative to bring the summer Olympic Games to New York City.

Ross is chairman of Equinox Holdings and chairman emeritus of New York's Real Estate Board (REBNY), the city's leading association of real estate business. Ross was involved in planning a major renovation of the iconic Frank Lloyd Wright building and other new museums as a member of the Solomon R. Guggenheim Foundation's board of trustees. He is a trustee of the New York Presbyterian Hospital, the Urban Land Institute, the NY Chapter of the International Juvenile Diabetes Research Foundation, the Levin Institute and a director of the Jackie Robinson Foundation and the World Resources Institute. He is also a member of the Executive Committee and a trustee of the Lincoln Center.

Ross was a major supporter and contributor to Mitt Romney's 2012 presidential campaign. He serves on the Cornell Tech Campus Board, a $2B redevelopment of Roosevelt Island, including the Joan & Irwin Jacobs Technion-Cornell Institute, a partnership between Cornell University and Technion –Israel Institute of Technology, which, once completed, will house a partnership between Cornell University and Technion.

The Dolphins Under Ross

During the 11 years of his ownership, the Dolphins have been terrible, making the playoffs only twice. They have been stuck in a series of completely middle of the road season, never winning much, and never tanking in order to rebuild. With a collection a truly "Meh" talent, and a recent reorganization from their franchise Quarterback Ryan Tannehill, the Dolphins will most likely be trying to catch fire with an early QB Pick in 2019, with an eye for rebuilding in the future.

THE BUFFALO BILLS OWNER TERRY PEGULA

Terrence Michael "Terry" Pegula (born March 27, 1951) is an American multi-billionaire with business interests in the development of natural gas, real estate, entertainment and professional sports. He is the owner of Pegula Sports and Entertainment, which includes, among other things, full ownership of the National Hockey League's Buffalo Sabres (NHL) and the National Football League's Buffalo Bills (NFL) along with his wife Kim Pegula.

On February 18, 2011 Pegula was quoted as saying, "Starting today, the reason for the existence of the Buffalo Sabres will be to win a Stanley Cup." The Sabres purchase included their National Lacrosse League counterpart, the Buffalo Bandits, who won four NLL championships. In May 2011, Pegula began negotiations on behalf of the Sabres to re-buy the Rochester Americans, who served as an affiliate of the Sabres American Hockey League from 1979 to 2008 (and was owned by the Sabres from 1979 to 1996); the deal was concluded at the end of June 2011. Upgrades to the team's arena, the Blue Cross Arena, came along with buying the Americans.

On September 9, 2014, it was announced that Pegula had placed a winning binding bid to purchase Buffalo Bills from the National Football League, a team that was placed on sale after the death of Ralph Wilson, the original owner and team founder. Pegula was a favorite among most local Bills fans and local politicians to purchase the team because of his commitment to Western New York. He ran against the future U.S. President Donald Trump and musician Jon Bon Jovi, the latter supported by the team's Maple Leaf Sports and Entertainment headquarters in Toronto. It was reported that the Pegulas made a $1.4 billion bid, all in cash.

On 17 September 2014, the Pegulas were unanimously approved by the finance committee of the NFL and were then scheduled to be presented for final owner approval at the NFL owners meeting on 8 October 2014. The Pegulas received unanimous approval from the owners of the league on 8 October and closed the deal on 10 October. Pegula's first major business order was to put an end to the Bills Toronto Series, which he did in an agreement reached on 3 December 2014. On the purchase of the Bills, Pegula and his wife introduced One Buffalo, a marketing campaign that has since evolved into a brand used across all their sports teams and related products. This made the Beauts the first non-league-owned NWHL team, North America's first professional women's hockey team owned by the same person who owned the NHL team on the market and got Pegula into women's hockey.

In 2018, Pegula reached an agreement to purchase the National Lacrosse League's Rochester Knighthawk's intellectual property in the fall of 2019. Curt Styres, owner of the Rochester Sports Group, orchestrated the sale as he planned to move his staff and roster to a new Halifax NLL team which was set to debut in the winter of 2020.

Terry Pegula built his wealth around the Oil and Gas Industries. Working for a time with Getty Oil and Felmont Oil Co., Pegula founded East Resources, a natural gas drilling company with $7,500 from family and friends. It greatly benefited from the discovery of deep natural gas layers in the Marcellus Formation and the development of the hydraulic fracturing ("fracking") recovery process. Pegula eventually sold the company's Pennsylvania, New York, and Rocky Mountain assets to Royal Dutch Shell for approximately $4.7 billion. Pegula is the KeyBank Center and Blue Cross Arena operator as well. Pegula purchased 79 Perry Street near KeyBank Center in 2017 and partnered with Labatt USA to redevelop the building into a mixed-use facility including a small test brewery called the "Labatt Brew House" and restaurant called "The Draft Room," as well as the U.S. headquarters of Labatt, the headquarters of Pegula Sports and Entertainment, and residential space.

Pegula also owns a share of the independent country music label Black River Entertainment. The label includes acts like Kelsea Ballerini, Kellie Pickler and Craig Morgan as well as the related Black River Publishing and Sound Stage Studio all under the Nashville, Tennessee-based Black River label. Impact Sports Performance is also under the umbrella of Pegula, two high-performance athletic training facilities based in Boca Raton, Florida and Buffalo's HarborCenter. Pegula also owns 716 Food and

Sport, a two-story sports theme-based restaurant that serves as Harbor Center's main business tenant. Through a partnership with Southern Tier Brewing Company, Pegula launched a branded "One Buffalo" craft beer that sells in all Pegula-owned properties and elsewhere in the region. The One Buffalo brand was also extended to the flavor of Perry's Ice Cream (which had already licensed Bills and Sabres theme flavors before Pegula's team purchases) and premium cupcakes, both formulated by Perry's Ice Cream (which had already licensed themed flavors before Pegula's team purchases).

An alumnus of Pennsylvania State University (Penn State), Pegula donated $102 million for the construction of the on-campus Pegula Ice Arena in 2010. As a result, the Penn State Nittany Lions, which had fielded club teams in both men's and women's hockey for years, would be able to transition both teams into NCAA Division I starting in the 2012–13 season. This resulted in a domino effect across the landscape of the men's college hockey. Because six Big Ten Universities now had men's hockey programs in Division I (the minimum number of teams required for official conference sponsorship under Big Ten bylaws and also the minimum required for a conference to be an automatic post-season qualifier), it was announced that Minnesota, Wisconsin, Michigan, Michigan State and Ohio State would join Penn State at the Big Ten Hockey Conference. Together with former WCHA members St. Cloud State, Minnesota-Duluth, Denver, Colorado College, Nebraska-Omaha, and North Dakota, Miami University and Western Michigan

University joined the upstart National Collegiate Hockey Conference. Notre Dame, a former CCHA member, joined Hockey East, which in 2014 recruited UConn from the Atlantic Hockey Association to start playing in Hockey East. The ECAC was the only Division I conference not affected by the major conference realignment after the dust settled. Because the arrival of Penn State gave the Big Ten only four varsity women's hockey programs, that conference was unable to add the sport, which meant that the women's hockey landscape did not undergo the radical changes that took place in the men's game. The women's Penn State team has settled in College Hockey America, a league that only sponsors women's hockey.

The Pegulas donated $12 million for the construction of the Kerr-Pegula Athletic Complex to Houghton College in Houghton, New York, of which Kim Pegula is an alumna. The facility includes new baseball and softball stadiums as well as a 115,000 square foot field house with a 200-meter eight-lane track, five tennis courts, weight room, cardiac fitness center and locker rooms. The new facility is primarily aimed at intercollegiate athletics at Houghton College, which has recently moved to Division III Athletics and the Empire 8 Conference. It opened on October 4, 2014.

Born in Carbondale, Pennsylvania, Pegula attended high school at Scranton Preparatory School. From there he attended college at Penn State University where he graduated in petroleum and natural gas engineering with a

Bachelor of Science degree. He was based in Allegany, New York, at the beginning of 1985. He currently lives in Boca Raton, Florida, together with his second wife, Kim Pegula (Kerr's maiden name), a graduate of Houghton College, whose home town is Fairport, New York. Kim was born in Seoul, South Korea, and at age 5 was adopted in 1973 by Ralph and Marilyn Kerr. He has five children, two from a previous marriage (Michael and Laura) and three with Kim (Jessica, Kelly and Matthew). Jessica Pegula is a tennis player on the Women's Tennis Association's Pro Circuit. Pegula owns a large yacht, christened *Top Five*..

The Bills under the Pegulas.

Although there has been a recent uptick in excitement over the Bills and their fanbase, including their limping into the playoffs in 2017, they continue to remain to be one of the worst teams in the National Football League. Consistently unable to find marquee players, they remain in sports purgatory. Unwillingness of players to play in small town tundra Buffalo can be most recently exemplified by Antonio Brown refusing a trade there, and instead settling with the soon to be Las Vegas Raiders.

PATRIOTS OWNER ROBERT KRAFT

Born on June 5, 1941, Robert Kenneth Kraft is an American businessman. He is Kraft Group's chairman and chief executive, a diversified holding company with assets in paper and packaging, sports and entertainment, real estate development, and a portfolio of private equity. He is the owner of New England Patriots from the National Football League, New England Revolution from the Major League Soccer, and Gillette Stadium, where both teams are playing.

Kraft was born in Brookline, Massachusetts, the son of Sarah Bryna (Webber) and Harry Kraft. Robert grew up in Brookline, where he attended Edward Devotion School and graduated from Brookline High School in 1959, where he served as Senior Class Chairman. At high school Kraft was unable to participate in most sports because it interfered with his Hebrew post-school studies and Sabbath observance. Kraft attended Columbia University, where he earned high honors. He considered running against the 3rd Congressional District Representative Philip J. Philbin of Massachusetts in 1970, but chose not to, citing the loss of privacy and the strain that would have caused his family to enter politics. He was further discouraged from entering politics by his friend's suicide, State Representative H. James Shea, Jr.

Kraft began his professional career with the Rand-Whitney Group, a Worcester-based packaging company run by his father-in-law Jacob Hiatt. In 1968, he gained control of the company through a leveraged buyout. He is still the chairman of this company. A trader of physical paper commodities, he founded International Forest Products in 1972. The two combined companies make up the United States ' largest private holding of paper and packaging companies. Kraft claimed to have started the company from a hunch that the increase in international communications and transportation would lead to an expansion of global trade in the late twentieth century. In 1997, International Forest Products became the top 100 U.S. exporters / importers and in 2013 was ranked No. 20 in that category in the Journal of Commerce.

In 1974, Kraft and five others purchased World Team Tennis (WTT) Boston Lobsters. The group spent heavily attracting a number of top players, including Martina Navratilova, and the Lo Lobsters. After the 1978 season, Kraft announced that the franchise would fold. After the Lobsters folded, Kraft was also mentioned as a bidder for the Boston Red Sox and the Boston Celtics.

In 1985, Kraft bought a 10-year option on Foxboro Raceway, a horse track adjacent to Schaefer Stadium in Foxboro, MA. The purchase prevented Patriots owner Billy Sullivan from holding non-Patriot events during races at Sullivan Stadium. Kraft took advantage of the fact that the Sullivans owned the stadium, but not the surrounding land. It was the beginning of a quest to buy not only the stadium, but also the Patriots. The Sullivan family was reeling from a series of bad investments, mainly The Jackson Five 1984 Victory Tour, for which they had to pledge Sullivan Stadium as collateral. These problems ultimately forced Sullivan to sell the team's controlling interest in 1988, while the stadium went bankrupt in 1988. The stadium was considered outdated and almost worthless, but the purchase included the lease of the stadium to the Patriots running through 2001. While Kraft also placed a bid on the Patriots franchise, he lost Victor Kiam's bid. The lease was ironclad enough to put an end to Sullivan's three-decade involvement with the Patriots. Kraft refused to let them break the lease when he and Kiam tried to move the team to Jacksonville. As a result, when Kiam was almost destroyed by his own bad investments, he was forced to sell the Patriots to James Orthwein. Since Orthwein purchased the team in 1992, there have been constant rumors that he wanted to move the Patriots to St. Louis. In 1994, at what was now Foxboro Stadium, Orthwein offered Kraft $75 million to purchase the rest of the team's lease. Had Kraft accepted Orthwein's offer, the last major hurdle to move the team would have been cleared. Kraft, however, turned it down. By 1994, Orthwein was not interested in long-term operation of the New England team and decided to sell it. Any prospective buyers had to deal with Kraft because of the terms of the operating covenant. With this in mind, Kraft made an offer that Orthwein accepted for an outright $172 million purchase from the team. It was the highest price ever paid for an NFL team at the time. Years later, Kraft said his passion for the Patriots led him in his pursuit of the team to "break each of my financial rules." Kraft stated that he keeps a Victory Tour poster among his memories as a reminder of what enabled him to fulfill his long-standing dream of becoming a major league team owner. Following the approval of the sale by the NFL, the Patriots sold their entire 1994 season–the first full sellout in franchise history. Since then, every home game–including pre-season, regular season, and playoffs –has been sold out.

In 1998, Kraft considered moving the Patriots to Hartford, Connecticut, based on an offer that Connecticut would fund a new downtown stadium. Kraft ended the deal on 30 April 1998 just before it became binding, choosing instead to build a new stadium in Foxboro with Massachusetts infrastructure funding from the Commonwealth. In 2002 Kraft privately funded a $350-million stadium for the Patriots, initially called the CMGI Field (later renamed Gillette Stadium). In 2007 Kraft began to develop the land around Gillette. The development included "Raytheon's Hall at Patriot Place," a multi-story museum and fame hall attached to the stadium, and the "CBS Scene," a CBS-themed restaurant. The Patriots experienced newfound and sustained success under Kraft's ownership. While under their original owners, the Sullivans, the Patriots appeared in Super Bowl XX, this was one of only six playoff appearances in 34 years. However, since Kraft bought the team, they made the playoffs in 23 years 18 times. They won AFC East titles in 1996, 1997, 2001, 2003, 2004, 2005, 2006, 2007, 2009, 2010, 2011, 2012, 2013, 2014, 2015, 2016, 2017, 2018 and 2019; they represented AFC in the Super Bowl finishing each of the following seasons: 1996 (lost), 2001 (won), 2003 (won), 2004 (won), 2007 (lost), 2011 (lost), 2014 (won), 2016 (won), 2017 (lost) and 2018 (won).

The Patriots finished the seasons of 2003, 2004, 2010 and 2016 with the same 14–2 regular-season records–having never won more than 11 games before Kraft purchased the team–and finished the regular season of 2007 at 16–0 before losing to the New York Giants in Super Bowl XLII. Kraft was mainly involved in the NFL labor negotiations of 2011. NFLPA representative and Indianapolis Colts Center Jeff Saturday praised Kraft for his role in the negotiations, saying, "Without him, this deal is not done... he is a man who helped us save football."

In 2005, it was reported that Russian President Vladimir Putin took one of Kraft's three Super Bowl rings. Kraft issued a statement promptly saying he gave Putin the ring out of "respect and admiration" he had for the Russian people and Putin's leadership. Kraft later said his earlier statement was not true, and had been issued under pressure from the White House. The ring is on display with state gifts at the Kremlin.

The Patriots Under Kraft

Arguable the greatest owner of all time, overseeing the greatest dynasty of all time, Kraft's success is unequaled in the forum of Professional Football. Although not without many controversies along the way. The level of unbelievable success that Patriots have obtained since the turn of the century may never be replicated again.

AFC NORTH

PITTSBURGH STEELERS OWNER ARTHUR ROONEY II

Rooney was born in Pittsburgh, Pennsylvania, the eldest of nine children of Patricia (Reagan) and long-time chairman of Steelers, Dan Rooney, and the grandson of Steelers founder, Art Rooney, Sr. He graduated with a B.A. from Pittsburgh University in 1978. He then attended the School of Law at the University of Duquesne, where he received his J.D. Degree in 1982. In May 2003, Rooney was appointed Team Chairman. Prior to that, he served as Steeler's Vice Chairman and General Counsel and has served on the Steelers Board of Directors since 1989. He presently serves as chairman of the NFL Stadium Committee and serves on various NFL boards, including the Legislative Committee, the Executive Committee of the Management Council, the International Committee and the Digital Media Committee.Prior to his father's death in 2017, Rooney II retained a 30% interest in the Steelers franchise and was in line with inheriting most of the 30% available share. He is one of only two managers of the league in the third generation, the other being John Mara, to whom he is linked by marriage (Mara's son is married to Rooney's sister, and both managers count actors Rooney Mara and Kate Mara as nieces.)

He presently maintains an office of counsel with Buchanan Ingersoll & Rooney law firm. He is active in the society of Pittsburgh, devoting considerable time to different organisations. He presently serves on the boards of the Pittsburgh Public Theatre, Saint Vincent College, Senator John Heinz Western PA History Center and United Way of America.

The Steelers Under Rooney

It goes without saying that the Steelers are one of if not the greatest NFL Franchise it its History, and Rooney has kept the excellence going through the Third Generation of his family. Recent locker room strife and the loss of major free agents Antonio Brown as well as the tumultuous hold out and release of Le'Veon Bell have plagued the team recently, but there is no reason to believe that the Steelers string of excellence will come to an end anytime soon.

CLEVELAND BROWNS OWNER JIMMY HASLAM

James Arthur Haslam III (born March 9, 1954) is the CEO of the Pilot Flying J Truck stop chain and, together with his spouse, Dee is the co-owner of the National Football League's Cleveland Browns and the co-owner of the Major League Soccer Columbus Crew SC. The Pilot Corporation was established in 1958 as the Pilot Oil Corporation by his dad, fellow businessman Jim Haslam.

Haslam, who lives in his native Knoxville, Tennessee, is the elderly brother of Bill Haslam, the former Governor of Tennessee. He is married to Susan 'Dee' Bagwell Haslam, CEO of RIVR Media. They have three adult kids, James Oakley (from the first marriage of Dee), Whitney Haslam Johnson, Cynthia Haslam Arnholt, and five grandchildren.

While attending Tennessee University, Haslam was Bob Corker's roommate, who became Tennessee's U.S. Senator. He is a member of the fraternity of Sigma Chi. In 1976, Haslam started his career at the Pilot Corporation. Haslam was appointed Vice President of Sales, Development and Operations in 1980. At that moment, with annual fuel sales of about 125 million gallons, Pilot operated 100 convenience stores. In 1981, Pilot opened its first travel center and by 1996–the same year that Haslam was appointed President and Chief Executive Officer–the firm had 96 travel centers and 50 convenience shops, with a combined oil sales of 1.2 billion gallons. In 2001, when Pilot Corporation joined Marathon Ashland Petroleum LLC to create Pilot Travel Centers LLC, it reached another milestone.

Pilot Corporation announced in 2008 that CVC Capital Partners had purchased an interest of 49.8 percent in Pilot Travel Centers LLC, facilitating the sale of its interest in Pilot Travel Centers by Marathon Petroleum Company (formerly Marathon Ashland Petroleum). Pilot Corporation maintained 50% ownership of Pilot Travel Centers LLC. All the shares of CVC Capital Partners in the business were purchased by the Haslam family in 2015.

Pilot's convenience shop activities remain Pilot Corporation's full ownership. Pilot Travel Centers LLC entered Flying J Inc in 2010. Pilot Flying J purchased Western Petroleum in 2012 and Maxum Petroleum's majority ownership and established Maxum Enterprises LLC, d / b / a Pilot Logistics Services in 2012. Pilot Logistics Services merged into Pilot Thomas Logistics in 2014 with Thomas Petroleum. One of the fastest increasing energy logistics businesses in North America is the Pilot Flying J subsidiary Pilot Thomas Logistics.

Pilot Flying J is one of America's biggest top 10 private holders and employs more than 24,000 people. The Pilot

Flying J network offers access to more than 70,000 truck parking spaces, 4,800 showers and 4,300 diesel lanes with DEF at the pump for clients.

The FBI executed a search warrant and affidavit in April 2013 detailing the Pilot Flying J chain's five-year fraud scheme. The firm paid customer restitution and agreed to pay a penalty of $92 million pursuant to a Criminal Enforcement Agreement. The civic participation of Haslam involves service on the Anderson Media Corporation board of directors. He has also served on the boards of Greater Knoxville's United Way, Knoxville's Lakeshore Park, and the National Truck Stop Operators Association (NATSO). Furthermore, Haslam served as honorary secretary of the Cleveland campaign commission for Boys & Girls Clubs and as campaign secretary for Knox Area Rescue Ministries and Greater Knoxville's United Way.

In 2006, he served as Tennessee Statewide Campaign Chair for U.S. Senator Bob Corker and in 2012 he served as Statewide Chairman of Finance for Tennessee Governor Bill Haslam, his brother. Haslam was inducted into the 2007 East Tennessee Business Hall of Fame Junior Achievement, and in 2010, he was named recipient of the Ernst & Young Entrepreneur Of The Year Award for the Tennessee Business Hall of Fame. In 2013, Haslam was awarded the Distinguished Alumnus Award by the University of Tennessee. He is the co-founder of the University of Tennessee's Haslam Scholars Program for Premier Honorary Students.

In 2008, Haslam acquired a minority interest in the Pittsburgh Steelers. He reached a deal with Browns owner Randy Lerner in 2012 to buy the $1 billion franchise. Forbes magazine valued the Browns at $977 million in 2011 which was 20th in the NFL. NFL rules prohibit ownership in various teams and so Haslam divested his stake in the Steelers.

The acquisition of the Browns by Haslams was unanimously approved by the 32 owners of the NFL on 12 October; the sale itself closed thirteen days later. Haslam has had a 21-75-1 record as team proprietor since formally taking over the Browns seven seasons ago in the 2012 season.

The Brown under Haslam

As listed above, the Browns have been mired in terrible mediocrity since Haslam's ownership, however there is hype and hope on the horizon. Since a notable appearance on HBO's 2018 version of Hard Knocks, the Browns have increasingly gained momentum and seem poised for their first playoff appearance since way back in 2003.

A league basement dweller, the team improved by firing perennial bumbling underperforming coach Hue Jackson, and turning to QB Baker Mayfield to be the face of the franchise and finally turn them around. After the acquisition of Odell Beckham in the 2019 offseason, the team appears poised to seize the division. On the other hand, they are the Browns and have let their fanbase down for decades now. The intent and improved buzz around the Browns in achievement enough, and it looks as those they are poised for a winning run in 2019 and beyond.

CINCINNATI BENGALS OWNER MIKE BROWN

Michael Brown (born August 10, 1935) is an executive of American football and the proprietor of the National Football League (NFL) Cincinnati Bengals, a position he has held since 1991. Co-founder and initial coach of the Cleveland Browns and Bengal's son, Paul Brown, entered the league with the Bengals when they were founded in 1968 and took over the squad after the death of his father.

Brown's ownership has been criticized for absence of on-field achievement, reluctance to cede football activities to a general manager, and connection between the team and Hamilton County to finance Paul Brown Stadium before and after a vote-approved tax rise.

Brown is Paul Brown's only living son. His brother, Pete, was the Senior Vice-President of Bengal's player staff until his death in 2017. His older brother, Robin, died of cancer in 1978. Brown graduated from Dartmouth College in 1957, where he played quarterback for their football team, and from Harvard Law School in 1959. In an unusual meeting between future sports owners, eventual New York Yankees owner George Steinbrenner hired him to a summer job as a deckhand for Kinsman Marine Transit Company.

The Bengals, then an American Football League team, were established by Paul Brown in 1968. (Several years after Paul Brown was rejected as Cleveland Browns head coach in a well-publicized Art Model controversy.) Mike started his executive responsibilities with the Bengals as assistant general manager. In addition to staff choices, he was a team spokesperson on problems of league regulations and team policy. He took over the team ownership duties after the death of his father in August 1991 and has since stayed in the ownership role. His first important step as owner was to fire famous coach Sam Wyche after the 1991 season (although he initially claimed that Wyche had resigned). Days later, Brown recruited Dave Shula as head coach, making Shula (at that moment) the second youngest NFL head coach in history, making Dave and Don Shula the first father-son to lead various NFL teams in the same year.

Brown mired himself in controversy when he started talks to build a new Stadium for the Bengals. Initially, Brown dismissed proposals from other towns to discuss moving the team. By 1995, he felt the tiny seating capacity of Riverfront Stadium and the absence of luxury boxes hampered the success of the Bengals. In 1995, he announced that Cincinnati had violated its lease contract by paying $167,000 in concession receipts late in one week. In 1996, electors from Hamilton County approved a one-half percent sales tax rise to finance the construction of a new facility for the Bengals and a second new facility for the Major League Baseball Cincinnati Reds. In 2000, the Bengals lodged a lawsuit against the County for the right to handle it. County managers agreed to allow a Bengals subsidiary to operate the stadium and it was opened later that year. In 2007, a county commissioner named Todd Portune thought that revenue released between 1995 and 1999 contradicted Brown's financial distress allegations. Ultimately, the Hamilton County Board of Commissioners was replaced as the plaintiff in the case. Fans supporting Portune quote what they feel is the broken promise that the Bengals would "be more competitive" with a fresh stadium. The Bengals had only seven out of 16 winning seasons since the stadium opened.

Rick Eckstein, co-author of "Public Dollars, Private Stadiums," defines the Hamilton County agreement as "the most lopsided stadium agreement since 1993". A 2008 Forbes study indicates that the team's direct revenue rankings have fallen since the building of the stadium. In 2010, the squad set a record for the fewest matches required to lose 200 under one particular owner. The Bengals retain a number of dismal records for Brown's ownership time frame: it is the only team with three nine-or-more losing streaks.It also maintains six out of twenty-five 0-6 starts (24%) and four out of thirteen 0-6 starts.

Marvin Lewis, who is the only head coach under Brown to have winning seasons, playoff appearances, division titles, and a total winning record at 131-129-3 (.504), is the most effective coach during Mike Brown's tenure. Under Lewis, however, all seven of the Bengals postseason appearances ended in first-round losses. Eventually the mediocrity claimed Lewis' long term hold on the coaches seat in 2019.

In 2009, Yahoo sports ranked Mike Brown as the NFL's second worst owner. Besides being the majority owner, Brown is also regarded the de facto general manager of the Bengals. He is one of two NFL managers with either the general manager's title or powers, the other being Jerry Jones from Dallas.

The Cincinnati Enquirer published information of testimony in a trial on Austin Knowlton's $300 million property in Hamilton County Probate Court in 2009. Brown testified that he got a general manager bonus each year since taking over the team in 1991. Because of the record of the team under his possession, Brown was criticized for his attitude to running the organization's football side.

However, since 2009, Brown has mainly relinquished day-to-day control over football issues to a committee made up of executive vice president Katie Blackburn (Brown's daughter), head coach Marvin Lewis, and several other Brown family members. This coincided with the return to respectability of the Bengals; since 2009 they have made the playoffs in all but two seasons.

Off-field behavior has remained one of the stains on the franchise. In the mid-to-late 2000s, the Bengals have been engaged with a variety of players in a series of disciplinary policies. In 2005, Chris Henry and Odell Thurman were drafted by the Bengals, each considering extremely talented but possible disciplinary risks during their university careers. They were among nine Bengal players detained for multiple crimes the following year. Brown cut several "problem players" in 2008, including Henry and Thurman, but re-signed Henry later that year. This came after five arrests and of Henry and Brown's the declaration of Henry and Brown's previously in the year that Henry's "behavior could no longer be tolerated." One fan protested by buying an electronic billboard along the Cincinnati border reading" CHRIS HENRY AGAIN? ARE YOU SERIOUS?". Henry died during a domestic dispute on December 17, 2009. Commenting on his death, Brown defended his decision to re-sign Henry, noting that "we knew him differently from his public persona." Posthumously, it was found that Chris Henry suffered from a progressive degenerative brain disease known as Chronic Traumatic Encephalopathy or CTE. According to a research study by the West Virginia University, the CTE may have led to his troubled behavior and, ultimately, his death.

Brown argues to have reconsidered this stance in later years. Speaking of the second appearance of the squad on Hard Knocks, Brown said, "We have a different squad now than we had a couple of years ago. We want the public to see them. We believe they're nice individuals. We believe they're going to take the public, they're going to like them. It provides us a boost." Brown remarked that the present attitude of the league towards discipline is a shift from a previous" boys are gonna be boys " at Hard Knocks.

After several losing seasons, Brown is historically unwilling to fire staff. His first hire as head coach, David Shula, lost fifty games quicker than any NFL coach in history (69 games); Shula was recruited over Kansas City Chiefs defensive coordinator Bill Cowher, probably because Brown saw similarities with himself and Shula in the same way that their respective parents (Don Shula and Paul Brown) in many ways overshadowed them. Cowher would take the same offseason's head coaching role with the rival Pittsburgh Steelers and have a 22-9 career record against the Bengals, the most victories he would have against any squad as a head coach, including an 8-1 record against Shula. Cowher also beat the Bengals in the 2006 wild card game and went on to win that year's Super Bowl title. Shula's successor, Bruce Coslet, retired with a record of 21-39 in 2000; Brown still had to fire him.

Cincinnati's first winning seasons and postseason appearances during Brown's ownership came under head coach Marvin Lewis, who had a regular season record of 131-122-3 with the team. Brown was however criticized for continuing to maintain Lewis after all seven of the playoff matches they appeared in during Lewis' tenure were lost by the Bengals. Following five successive opening-round postseason losses from 2011 to 2015, a first in the NFL, and back-to-back losing seasons in 2016 and 2017, Lewis got a two-year contract extension, receiving severe criticism from the press and fans. When Brown and Lewis parted ways in 2018, the 16-year tenure of Lewis became the longest of any NFL head coach not to win a playoff match.

Brown also values the relationship between his family and the franchise; evident in his choice of naming Paul Brown Stadium after his dad rather than selling corporate naming rights to it. Daughter Katie Blackburn is the team's executive chairman and her husband Troy is a VP with additional members of the front office staff. From 1994-2000, the Bengals paid more than $50 million in salaries back to the Brown Family and various staff. On ABC's Monday Night Football, Esiason became a color analyst.

Brown employs a very tiny scouting staff. A 2008 comparison between the scouting department of the Bengals and five other AFC teams with a .540 + winning percentage since 1991 showed the winning teams employing five or more scouts, while the Bengals employed only one. Since then, two extra scouts have been added by the Bengals (Marvin Lewis initially claimed that when he was hired, Brown assured him of a retooled scouting staff).

Brown's emphasis on the quarterback made public his belief that a "bell cow" quarterback is a necessity to turn a squad into a winner. In a 1999 interview, he remarked, "If you don't have a productive quarterback, you won't go anywhere...I know it doesn't seem that easy, but it is." Comparing quarterbacks to other roles on a football team, Brown said," It's the wheel hub.

Brown rejected the then-Saints coach Mike Ditka's offer of nine draft picks for one in the NFL draft of 1999 against Coach Coslet's guidance from that time. Instead, Brown overruled Coslet and chosen University of Oregon quarterback Akili Smith. Smith only played 22 games in his NFL career and is ultimately considered to be a draft bust. Coslet later regretted that in trying to persuade Brown to accept the offer of the Saints he "didn't insist hard enough."

Before the 1992 Draft, press reports stressed the need for either a cornerback or a defensive linemen for the Bengals. Brown himself was quoted the day before the draft as saying, "We'd love to get a top defensive linemen, they're at a premium, and that's less true of other positions. Instead, the Bengals selected Houston quarterback David Klingler. Then Bengals quarterback Boomer Esiason and David Fulcher both publicly challenged the move the next day, arguing that the team had more important defensive needs. Klingler was later considered a bust.

Esiason has since revealed that, at the end of the 1991 season, he had genuinely requested a trade that might have caused Brown to pick Klingler (Esiason was traded to the New York Jets in 1993). Years later, Brown put a good deal of accountability on Carson Palmer, calling him the "lead dog" of the Bengals and saying "as he passes, we go". The Bengals were 46-51 (.474) starting with Palmer. Palmer threatened to retire from football if he was not traded by the Bengals during the offseason of 2011. Brown insisted that he would not "reward" Palmer's requirements, arguing that Palmer made a dedication to the organisation when it was awarded a contract extension. On 27 August 2011, Brown released Carson's younger brother, Jordan from the team. On 18 October 2011, the Bengals finally traded Carson Palmer to the Oakland Raiders for a 2012 first round draft pick and a conditional second round 2013. Brown's "a very, very, very stubborn guy", commented Palmer.

Andy Dalton was chosen in the 2011 NFL Draft and became the first QB in franchise history to lead the squad five years in a row to the playoffs, although the Bengals were eliminated every year in the first round. In what became the fifth consecutive loss due to injury, Dalton did not play in the postseason.

In 1998, punter Lee Johnson was cut by the Bengals. Brown attempted to fine Johnson after cutting him for "conduct detrimental to the team" in relation to comments Johnson had made about the organization and the 1998 season. A reporter asked Johnson after a Bengals loss "if you were a fan, would you have come here today?" to which Johnson replied "No, no way...why would you? You're saying (losing) is OK. I guess if you've got nothing else to do. I'd sell my tickets." This fine resulted in a dispute with the NFL players union, whose counsel remarked "A fine is a disciplinary measure, you discipline someone to try and make sure they're a better employee in the future. How can you do that if you've fired them?"

In 2000, the Bengals instituted a "loyalty clause," which allows the Bengals to deny various bonuses to players depending on the remarks they make about the Bengals. The ability to enact such a clause appears justified under the collective bargaining agreement which states an NFL team can fine a player one week's salary and suspend him without pay for up to four weeks for any action the club considers detrimental to the team. Brown responded that the clause would only be enacted under extreme circumstances. He wrote an article for the Cincinnati Enquirer, quoting team cohesion as his primary motivation for the clause. The "Carl Pickens Clause" from the 2000 offseason is often described as an example. Brown renewed Bruce Coslet's contract despite his 21–36 Bengals record. Pickens answered, "I don't know. We're going to win; we're going to turn this around here. And they're bringing (Coslet) back." Pickens ended his career with the Tennessee Titans.

Over the years since the clause, Bengals players have commented on a negative atmosphere within the organization, notably Takeo Spikes, Jeff Blake, and Jon Kitna. The most vocal critic of the Bengals since the clause was instituted was Corey Dillon. In 2001, after becoming the sixth player in NFL history to rush for 1,000 yards or more in five consecutive seasons, he remarked, "at the end of the season, what do I have to feel good about? Nothing at all. It's not cool." After a fifth losing season with the team in 2002, he remarked, ""I'm tired of it, six years of this B.S. I don't lie to you. I'm tired of this shit, period." At the end of the 2003 season, Dillon requested a trade after throwing most of his equipment to the fans during the last home match of the season. In the following season, he went on to win a Super Bowl with the New England Patriots.

Brown has also garnered quite a reputation for dogmatic frugality during his tenure as owner. In 1994, agent Leigh Steinberg described Brown as "in a lonely struggle for economic rationality in the NFL" and "a figure like Don Quixote pushing back the forces of wage folly." Over the years, Brown has proved unwilling to complete free agent signatures or trades. Recent examples are Warren Sapp (2004), Shaun Rogers (2008), and Johnathan Joseph (2011).

Agent Drew Rosenhaus described it as a "matter of hours" before the Bengals signed Sapp, only a day before the Raiders signed him. Sapp accused the Bengals of "playing with the cash" on the initial deal they offered him, with more cash being deferred to incentives rather than guarantees. The Associated Press reported on 29 February 2008 that there was a completed trade between Cincinnati and the Detroit Lions for Rogers. However, the trade fell through and the following day it was confirmed that instead the Lions traded Rogers to the Cleveland Browns.

MikeBrownSucks organizers organized a boycott of a regular season game in December 2001 and fans visiting this site as well as another site, SaveTheBengals.com, paid for aircraft flying a banner in the Cincinnati area calling for Brown's resignation. Who Dey Revolution (WDR) has staged "Project Mayhem" since 2008 in an attempt to convince Brown to create adjustments to the Bengals. These steps ranged from calling the Bengal "JERK line" to reporting Brown's behavior as abusive, to buying billboards showing a request for a new General Manager, to goods and ticket donations / boycotts and letter-writing campaigns. Buying and distributing 1000 urinal cakes at a home match in Bengal advertised Brown's regular season record of 98–188 for life.

The Bengals stayed popular within Cincinnati despite these demonstrations. A November 21, 2010 game vs. the Buffalo Bills marked the first time since November '03 that network affiliates and DirectTV were legally forced to "black out" the Bengals game within Paul Brown Stadium's 75-mile radius due to absence of ticket sales. The remaining home matches were also blacked out against the New Orleans Saints, Cleveland Browns, and San Diego Chargers. The squad sold out 57 straight matches before that, a club record.

In reaction to fan and media criticism, several individuals cast Brown as a sympathetic figure. Marvin Lewis tearfully granted the match ball to Brown after a surprising defeat by the Kansas City Chiefs in 2003 and told his players "he has put up with so much for you guys." For-

43

mer Bengals reject ideas that Brown is unconcerned about winning. Boomer Esiason, now a CBS analyst, relates to Brown as a "good person" who is merely over his head running the team. In 1998 interviews, radio analyst Cris Collinsworth and Bengals Dave Lapham also dismissed ideas that Brown was not interested in winning. Collinsworth remarked, "I don't believe anyone can suffer more than Mike is about this."

The Bengals Under Brown

A bumbling owner owing mostly to nepotism to get him where he is, Brown has remained stubborn in the face of his team's multi-decade failure. The definition of mediocrity under Marv Lewis, the team starts anew under new coach Zac Taylor in 2019. Although likely to remain competitive, they have a long road in 2019 in one of the toughest divisions in professional football. Because of all of this, they are likely to finish last and repeat their long march of mediocrity.

BALTIMORE RAVENS OWNER STEVE BISCIOTTI

Stephen J. Bisciotti (born 10 April 1960) is an American business manager and the present majority owner of the NFL's Baltimore Ravens. He established Aerotek, a home health and medical staffing company based in Columbia, Maryland, and co-founded Allegis Group, a global talent management company headquartered in Hanover, Maryland, owned by Aerotek

His dad died of cancer when he was eight years old. His maternal grandfather took over raising him after the death of his father. Bisciotti attended Severn School but left after two years and moved to Severna Park High School. He played on the football team in his senior year, although he said "I wasn't much of a high school athlete, but played football, baseball, and basketball all the time I grew up." In 1982, Bisciotti graduated with a degree in liberal arts from Salisbury State University in Maryland. A year later, at 23, he began Aerotek, a staffing firm in the aerospace and technology industries, with his cousin Jim Davis. Bisciotti and Davis, running the company from a second-hand machinery cellar, generated $1.5 million in revenues in the first year. Aerotek grew into the Allegis Group, which is now the biggest private employee corporation in the world. Bisciotti's participation in the sports business and purchasing a stake in the Baltimore Ravens brought more attention to its once low-profile company. He had an option in the agreement to buy the remaining 51 percent from Art Modell for $325 million in 2004. The NFL approved his purchase of the majority stake in the club on April 9, 2004. One of the first projects directed by Bisciotti as owner of the Ravens was to build the state-of-the-art training and practice facility of the team, dubbed "The Castle," which opened in October 2004.

Bisciotti fired legendary coach Brian Billick after the 2007 season, although Billick's eight years as the Ravens ' head coach included the team's victory in Super Bowl XXXV. He then amazed many critics by choosing John Harbaugh as his new manager, despite Harbaugh's peak of prior experience as a one-year defensive back coach after several productive years as the Philadelphia Eagles' special teams coach.

In 2012, the Baltimore Ravens capitalized on a 10-6 season to continue to win Super Bowl XLVII against the San Francisco 49ers on February 3, 2013. In 2005, Bisciotti ranked 378 among the Forbes 400, a list of the richest Americans. In 2009, Aerotek, co-founded by Bisciotti, achieved a $1.2 million settlement in a class action lawsuit lodged on behalf of more than 1,000 Aerotek employees working at a call center for Verizon Internet Services in Martinsburg, West Virginia, which was closed in December 2006. The firm was then prosecuted to settle allegations that, according to Berkeley County Circuit Court records, the employees were not paid in a timely manner for accrued personal time and not all of the salaries due under the West Virginia Wage Payment and Collection Act and the Fair Labor Standards Act.

The Ravens Under Biscotti

Since Biscotti initially acquired a minority stake in the Ravens in 2000, Baltimore has been one of the most consistent and difficult teams to match up against. Their two Super Bowl victories of 2000 and 2012 both carry the mark of a team notoriously hard-nosed on defense. The team ranks in an elite group including the Steelers and Patriots as one of the finest franchises in the NFL this Century.

AFC SOUTH

JACKSONVILLE JAGUARS OWNER SHAHID KHAN

Shahid "Shad" Khan is a Pakistani-American billionaire businessman, born on July 18, 1950. He is the owner of the National Football League (NFL) Jacksonville Jaguars, Fulham F.C. (From the English Football League Championships) and Professional Wrestling Promotion All Elite Wrestling (AEW) where he is the lead investor. Khan is also the proprietor of Flex-N-Gate in Urbana, Illinois, an automotive parts manufacturer.

Khan was featured on Forbes magazine's front cover in 2012, associating him with the American Dream. Khan's net worth as of May 2019 was $6.8 billion. He is ranked 65th in the Forbes 400 list of the richest Americans, and overall the 224th richest person in the world. He is also the richest person of Pakistani origin

Khan was born in Lahore, Pakistan, to a middle-class family engaged in the building industry. His mom was a mathematics professor. He moved to the United States at the age of 16 in 1967 to study at the University of Illinois in Urbana–Champaign. He spent his first night in a $2/night room at YMCA University when he moved to the United States, and his first task was to wash dishes for $1.20 an hour.

He graduated with a BS in Industrial Engineering from the UIUC College of Engineering in 1971. He was subsequently granted the Distinguished Alumni Award for Mechanical Science and Engineering much later in 1999. While attending the University of Illinois, he worked at the Flex-N-Gate Corporation. He was employed as the company's engineering manager when he graduated. He began Bumper Works in 1978, which produced vehicle bumpers for tailored pickup trucks and body shop repairs. The startup involved a $50,000 loan from the Small Business Administration and $16,000 of his savings. In 1980, he purchased Flex-N-Gate from his former employer, Charles Gleason Butzow, which brought Bumper Works to the fold. Khan grew the business to supply the Big Three car manufacturers with bumpers. In 1984, he started providing Toyota pickups with a tiny amount of bumpers. By 1987 it was the only provider for Toyota pickups and by 1989 it was the only provider in the United States for the entire Toyota line. Adopting The Toyota Way improved the effectiveness and capacity of the business to modify its manufacturing method in just a few minutes. Since then, the business has grown from $17 million in revenues to an estimated $2 billion in 2010. By 2011, Flex-N-Gate had 12,450 staff and 48 manufacturing facilities in the United States and several other countries and had income of $7.5 billion in 2017!

Khan's first attempt to buy a National Football League squad came on February 11, 2010, when he signed an agreement to buy 60 percent of the then-St. Louis Rams off Chip Rosenbloom and Lucia Rodriguez, subject to approval by other NFL owners. However, Stan Kroenke, the Rams minority shareholder, eventually exercised a clause in his ownership contract to match any suggested bid. On 29 November 2011, Khan decided to buy the Jacksonville Jaguars from Wayne Weaver and his ownership group subject to NFL approval. The terms of the agreement were not instantly revealed, other than a verbal engagement to keeping the team in Jacksonville, Florida. The purchase cost was estimated to be $760 million. On December 14, 2011, the purchase was unanimously approved by the NFL owners. The sale was completed on January 4, 2012 making Khan the first member of an ethnic minority to own an NFL team.

Khan negotiated the purchase of the Premier League's London soccer club Fulham from its former owner, Mohamed Al Fayed, in July 2013. The deal was finalized on July 12, 2013, with an estimated amount of £ 150–200 million. An official purchase price for the club was not announced to him saying that it was "extremely confidential. In 2019 it was disclosed that Khan was the lead investor behind the professional wrestling company, All Elite Wrestling alongside his son Tony, where he is the chairman.

Khan met Ann Carlson (now Ann Carlson Khan) at college in 1967 and dated her 10 years before they were married in 1977. Together they have two kids, their eldest son Tony Khan was born in 1982. In 1991, Shahid Khan became a naturalized American citizen.

The Jaguars Under Khan

Since buying the Jaguars in 2012, there has been constant rumour and speculation that they would move to London. In fact, they are often selected to play games annually at Wembley Stadium. However, this has not come to fruition and Khan has slowly evolved into one of the most colorful and loved owners in the league. Generally mediocre, the Jaguars put together a truly superior season in 2017 before tragically falling to the Patriots late in the AFC Championship that year.

INDIANAPOLIS COLTS OWNER JIM IRSAY

James Irsay (born on 13 June 1959) is the owner and CEO of the National Football League Indianapolis Colts.

Irsay was born in Lincolnwood, Illinois, son of Harriet (born Pogorzelski) and entrepreneur Robert Irsay in Chicago. His dad was from a Hungarian Jewish family and his mom was the daughter of Polish Catholic immigrants. Irsay was raised a Catholic and had no knowledge of the Jewish heritage of his father until he was fourteen. Jim's brother, Thomas, was born with a mental disability and died in 1999, and his sister, Roberta, died in a car accident in 1971. Irsay attended high school in Wilmette, Illinois, a suburb just south of Chicago, Illinois, and Mercersburg Academy in Mercersburg, Pennsylvania. After high school, he attended and graduated with a degree in broadcast journalism from Southern Methodist University in 1982. Irsay was playing linebacker as a walk-on for the SMU Mustangs football squad, but his playing career finished with an ankle injury.

Irsay was twelve years old when the Baltimore Colts were bought by his father, Robert Irsay. He entered the professional employees of the Colts after graduating from SMU in 1982. In 1984, one month after the Colts moved from Baltimore to Indianapolis, he was appointed Vice President and General Manager. Jim took on the position of Senior Executive Vice President, General Manager and Chief Operating Officer in April 1996 after his dad experienced a stroke in 1995. Jim participated in a legal fight with his stepmother over ownership of the team when his dad died in 1997, but later became the youngest NFL team owner at 37 at that time.

However, Irsay also lobbied to safeguard the NFL's image. In 2009, Irsay was vocal about stopping the purchase of the St. Louis Rams from a group that included talk show host Rush Limbaugh. "I wasn't even able to consider voting for him myself," Irsay said at a conference of NFL owners. "When comments are made that are inappropriate, incendiary and insensitive... our words do harm, and we don't need it." Irsay has made political donations to John Edwards and Harry Reid in the past.

In 1980, Irsay married Meg Coyle and the couple had three children, Carlie, Casey and Kalen. On 21 November 2013, after being separated since 2003, Meg filed for divorce. On 16 March 2014, Irsay was detained on suspicion of DUI and drug possession in Carmel, Indiana. According to Bob Kravitz, an Indianapolis Star sports reporter, Irsay had a continuing drug problem. This was highlighted when it was later disclosed that Irsay's mistress, Kimberly Wundrum, had overdosed and died in a house that Irsay had controversially bought with the Indianapolis Colts' corporate cash. Irsay's daughter, Carlie, took over the day-to-day operations of the Colts while he was in rehab. On September 2, 2014, shortly after pleading guilty to OWI and being sentenced to one year of probation, Irsay was suspended by the NFL for six games and fined $500,000. In 2001, Irsay bought the initial manuscript On the Road or otherwise known as "the scroll": a constant one hundred and twenty-foot scroll of sheets, which Jack Kerouac cut into size, taped together for $2.43 million. And on 5 May 2018, for an auction of $2.4 million, he acquired an initial printing of the original Alcoholics Anonymous book of 1939 with notes handwritten by AA co-founder Bill Wilson.

The Colts Under Irsay

Easily considering one of the more "Clown Owners" of the league, Irsay is known for being brash and outspoken and for his screw ups in his personal life. However, the Colts where a very mediocre team for decades before he took over as a young owner in 1997, and since then they have experienced stretches of absolute dominance including a Super Bowl victory in the 2006 season and another appearance in the 2010 season. With one of the most legendary Quarterbacks in League history in Peyton Manning at the helm for years during Irsay's tenure as owner, the Colts have seen their share of good times. Now with another dominant Quarterback in Andrew Luck, they hope to become great again, despite being just "good" for nearly a decade at this point.

TENNESSEE TITANS OWNER AMY ADAMS STRUNK

Amy Adams Strunk is an American businesswoman best known to be Bud Adams' daughter and inherited part of his fortune. She is now managing the Tennessee Titans and is an owner in the National Football League. Strunk owns one-third of the franchise, with the remaining two-thirds owned by other family members. The team is presently owned by the KSA Industries umbrella of companies, which is also further owned by many of the companies of Bud Adams. The position of Titans Owner belonged to her sister, Susie Adams Smith, whose husband Tommy Smith was team president and CEO, before Strunk took over as controlling shareholder in 2015.

Strunk attended Texas University, graduating with a history degree. Born into extreme riches, Strunk is also participated in the other companies of her family, including Bud Adams Ranches, Inc., as well as serving as the chairman of Kenada Fox Hounds, a fox hunting organisation, and the Little River Oil and Gas Company. Strunk's ownership began originally with an inherited third of the Titans stake at the death of her father, with another third going to her sister, Susie Adams Smith. After two tumultuous years with Smith as controlling owner, the family decided to transfer the mantle to Strunk, with Smith selling her interest in the team in 2017. Strunk was the representative proprietor of the Tennessee Titans during a league vote in 2015. In 2016, Strunk was appointed to the NFL Hall of Fame Committee and was also appointed to the Pro Football Hall Board of Trustees.

Thanks in big portion to the Titans 2018 uniform reveal event that Strunk primarily arranged in downtown Nashville, the NFL awarded Nashville the honor of hosting the 2019 NFL Draft.

Strunk is an enthusiastic equestrian and fox hunter. She is married to Bill Hunt, a former commercial airline pilot. They have homes in Waller, Texas and Nashville, Tennessee. From two prior marriages, she has three grown kids, Tracy Thompson, Tommy Thompson, and Blanche Strunk.

The Titans under Strunk

With such a short sample size, the jury is still out on the legacy of Strunk as an owner of the Titans. Getting the 2019 NFL Draft to Nashville is indeed a notable accomplishment, as the draft itself was the most built up NFL Draft spectacle yet. The Titans remain the definition of middling, never bad, never great, which a series of talented but never game breaking players and a slow boring offense. Anything can change in the future however.

HOUSTON TEXANS OWNERS BOB AND JANICE MCNAIR

Robert C. McNair (January 1, 1937–November 23, 2018) was an American entrepreneur, philanthropist and owner of the Houston Texans of the National Football League.

McNair grew up in Forest City, North Carolina, a town of about 7,500 in the foothills of Western North Carolina. He spent most of his twenties and thirties as a struggling sales professional and unsuccessful businessman whose companies failed. When he established the business Cogen Technologies, which he sold to Enron and CalPERS in 1999, he ultimately broke through to success. McNair maintained energy plant ownership in New York and West Virginia up until his death. McNair served as Chairman and CEO of The McNair Group, a Houston, Texas based economic and real estate property company. He was also the proprietor of the personal investment firm Palmetto Partners, Ltd., which manages the government and private equity investments of McNairs, and was chairman of the McNair Foundation. In June 2000, McNair created Cogene Biotech Ventures, a biotechnology investment firm, where he served as chairman of the business.

He was rumored to be interested in purchasing a soccer club

in the United Kingdom, and twice went to visit St Andrews, home of the Birmingham City F.C. Championship team, which has been on sale for the previous two years. A consortium led by McNair produced a bid to buy Reading F.C. on January 3, 2014 ultimately fell through.

Committed to returning the NFL to Houston City after the Oilers left the city in 1996 to become the Tennessee Titans, McNair established "Houston NFL Holdings" in 1998. The NFL announced on October 6, 1999 that McNair had been awarded the 32nd NFL franchise. This squad would become the Houston Texans who started playing in 2002. They won their first AFC South title in 2011, repeating in 2012 on their way to four titles in six seasons. In 2004 and 2017, he was instrumental in bringing two Super Bowls to Houston's NRG Stadium. On October 29, 2017, in a game against the Seattle Seahawks, the majority of the Texans' players knelt during the national anthem after McNair had commented about having the "inmates running the prison" during a league owner meeting regarding the ongoing protests by NFL players during the anthem. McNair had apologized, stating that he was not referring to the players, but rather to the "relationship between the league office and team owners." It was the first time a Texans player had knelt during the anthem.

McNair was a member of the Texas Business Hall of Fame and was a present or former member of the Board of Trustees of several institutions. On September 12, 2007, McNair gave $100 million to recruit top scientists and physicians from Baylor College of Medicine. He was a recipient of the Torch of Liberty Award from the Anti-Defamation League. McNair is a main supporter of the Horizons Leadership Institute of Sigma Chi. McNair donated over $1 million to complete McNair Field, which hosts a college summer wooden bat squad in the Coastal Plain League. The Home team is called the Forest City Owls. In the opening night of the stadium, McNair threw out the first pitch (May 29, 2008), and the Owls beat the Gastonia Grizzlies, 4–2, even turning a triple play! In 1998, at the University of South Carolina, the McNairs created the McNair Scholar Program. In 1999, Robert McNair obtained from the university an honorary doctorate in human letters.

The Robert and Janice McNair Educational Foundation was founded in 1989. The foundation's objective was to remove some of the economic obstacles that prevented Rutherford County High School students from attending college. The first recipients were the 1990 class. Around $2.6 million in financial aid has been given to date by the McNair Foundation.

The Robert and Janice McNair Foundation, founded in 2015, offers donations to establish business centers at colleges across the United States. The foundation set up learning centres for entrepreneurship at Columbia College, Northwood University, Houston Baptist University, St. Thomas University, and South Carolina University in September 2016, as well as a research center at the Baker Institute at Rice University.

Political contributions According to one count, McNair was the biggest donor of Senate Majority Leader Mitch McConnell from 1 January 2009 to 30 September 2015, contributing $1,502,500. He also donated to several candidates for the Republican Party.

McNair died on 23 November 2018. He was diagnosed with skin cancer in 1994 and was being treated for multiple types of cancer. In the last months of his life, he had mainly withdrawn from the activities of the team. McNair's spouse, Janice, became Texans' main owner, representing the team at owner's' conferences. His son, Cal, who was chief operating officer, became chairperson and chief operating officer of the franchise

The Texans Under the McNairs

Although Houston has a decent history of success in the NFL, much of it has to do with the Oilers in the past. McNair was clearly a visionary in bringing a franchise back to the 3rd largest city in the United States, but for years the Texans were truly the league's doormat, which fringe Hall of Fame players like Andre Johnson languishing there in practical anonymity. Recently however, while not dominant, the team has made the postseason more frequently and can flash on offense from time to time. Bringing the Lombardi trophy to Houston still seems at least a few years off for now...

AFC WEST

DENVER BRONCOS CEO JOE ELLIS (RUNNING THE FRANCHISE FOR PAT BOWLEN)

Josiah Wear Ellis (born 16 November 1958) is an American football administrator who is presently the National Football League (NFL)'s Denver Broncos Chairman and CEO.

Ellis graduated from Colorado College in 1980. He attended the L's graduate school. To receive his Master's degree, Kellogg School of Management at Northwestern University. Joe graduated from Northwestern in 1988. Ellis started his NFL career with the Denver Broncos as their marketing director. He served the league as Vice President of Club Administration and Stadium Management until joining the Broncos as their Executive Vice President of Business Operations in 1998 after acquiring his Masters degree. Joe had been acting for 10 years in this capacity. Joe then became the Chief Operating Officer of the team in 2008. For three seasons, he retained this role until January 5, 2011. He was elevated to the Denver Broncos' role as president after 13 years with the Denver Broncos organization. After

Owner Pat Bowlen had been diagnosed with Alzheimer's disease, Ellis took over leadership control of the franchise. Ellis lives with his spouse, Ann, in Denver, Colorado. They have three kids: two sons, Si and Zander, and a daughter, Catherine. Through his mom, Nancy Walker Bush Ellis, he is also a member of the Presidential Bush family.

Broncos Former Owner Pat Bowlen

Patrick Dennis Bowlen (February 18, 1944–June 13, 2019) was the National Football League (NFL) Denver Broncos' majority owner. The Bowlen family bought the squad from Edgar Kaiser in 1984, including his two brothers John Bowlen and Bill Bowlen, and sister Marybeth Bowlen. Bowlen served as CEO of Broncos from his acquisition of the club in 1984 until July 2014 when, owing to the start and advancement of Alzheimer's disease, he stepped down as CEO of Broncos.

Bowlen was raised in Prairie du Chien, Wisconsin. Bowlen later graduated from the University of Oklahoma with degrees in Business (1965) and Law (1968). During his time in Oklahoma, he played as a wide receiver for the Oklahoma Sooners Freshman Football Team as well as for the Edmonton Huskies Junior Football Team, where he was a member of two Canadian Junior Football League Championship Teams in 1962 and 1963. By becoming a successful lawyer in Edmonton, Alberta, Bowlen became rich in his own right. Bowlen also worked as an executive for the business of his father and as a developer of real estate and had significant investments in the mining sector. His building firm, Batoni-Bowlen Enterprises, constructed the Northlands Coliseum during his business career in Edmonton, which would be home to the Edmonton Oilers for 42 years.

Bowlen was an approved member of the International Brotherhood of Pi Kappa Alpha. Bowlen launched Chapter Beta Omicron in 1963 at the University of Oklahoma,. Bowlen was admitted to the bar in 1969 and was a member of the Alberta Law Society and the Canadian Bar Association. The Denver Broncos endured several legal fights against former owner Edgar Kaiser between 1999 and 2008. In 1998, Bowlen decided to sell a share in the team to John Elway, a retired football legend. When Bowlen let Kaiser slip the presence of the offer while both were at the Bohemian Grove in 1999, Kaiser sued, claiming a contract breach. Kaiser claimed that if any agreement concerning franchise ownership was made, he had the right of first refusal. A jury ruled in favor of Kaiser and a federal judge in 2004 decreed that Kaiser had the right to buy back 10 percent of the Broncos using the same conditions of purchase provided to Elway. Bowlen appealed the original verdict that ruled in favor of Kaiser and won in 2008, as the Court of Appeal ruled that the Bowlen-Elway deal structure did not violate the original right of first refusal. On 30 December 2008, Broncos head coach and vice president of Football Operations Mike Shanahan was fired by Bowlen after a 14-year term as head coach. Bowlen said his squad wished to go in a new direction. Bowlen spent two weeks searching for a fresh head coach and eventually chose Josh McDaniels, who was the New England Patriots" offensive coordinator at the moment. Subsequently, McDaniels was fired as the Broncos' head coach after a losing streak in the 2010 season. Bowlen appointed Brian Xanders as the sole general manager of the team on February 12, 2009 and fired Jim and Jeff Goodman.

Bowlen and the Broncos hired former Carolina Panthers' coach John Fox as their new head coach within two weeks of the end of the regular season 2010-11. Although Bowlen had conversations with Fox prior to the hiring, the hiring was largely the responsibility of fresh front-office executive John Elway. By early 2009, rumors had begun to emerge that Bowlen had stepped out of the spotlight due to short-term memory loss. He told The

Denver Post columnist Woody Paige that his memory wasn't what it used to be and that he couldn't recall details of the Broncos back-to-back Super Bowl titles in the late 1990s. Bowlen no longer played a significant part in the decision-making of the Broncos starting in 2010, and executive vice president John Elway and president Joe Ellis took over. On July 23, 2014, owing to complications with Alzheimer's illness, he formally relinquished control of the squad to Joe Ellis. On November 1, 2015, Bowlen was inducted into the Ring of Fame of the Broncos, earning him a bronze plaque standing on the southern side of the Sports Authority Field at Mile High. After Bowlen purchased the team in 1984, the Broncos briefly held the largest percentage winning position at Mile High. The New England Patriots had surpassed that figure at the time of Bowlen's death. Colorado Crush ownership Besides being the Broncos' owner and CEO, Bowlen was also a partner in the Colorado Crush of the Arena Football League. He shared ownership with Denver's Stan Kroenke sports mogul and iconic John Elway quarterback from Broncos. In 2003, the Crush joined the AFL as a franchise for development. The team became a perennial championship contender and one of the top franchises of the league after a 2–14 season in 2003. The Crush won the 2005 Championship of the Arena Football League.

In 2006, Major League Lacrosse decided to grow its team league by incorporating the Denver Outlaws. The Denver Outlaws has been Bowlen's most winning franchise ever, boasting a 69.0 percent regular season win proportion since its inception. The Outlaws went to the playoffs each year of their life except one (2015) and advanced eight times to the championship match (2006, 2008, 2009, 2012, 2014, 2016, 2017, and 2018), winning the championship in 2014, 2016, and 2018.

Bowlen was a member of the Board of Trustees of the University of Denver and contributed to the financing of the Pat Bowlen

Athletic Training Center on the campus of the school. He also made significant contributions to the local chapters of the Denver Boys & Girls Club.

Awards and honors Inducted to the Pro Football Hall of Fame (class of 2019) Three-time Super Bowl champion (as owner of the Denver Broncos) ArenaBowl XIX champion (as part owner of the Colorado Crush) Three-time champion of the Steinfeld Cup (as owner of the Denver Outlaws) Broncos Ring of Fame (class of 2015) Colorado Business Hall of Fame (class of 2015). On June 13, 2019, Bowlen died as a result of his long battle with Alzheimer's disease. Under terms set prior to Bowlen's death, Joe Ellis will lead a three-person trust representing his estate; Bowlen's intent was for his children to inherit the franchise, though he did not specify which of his children would have first right.

The Broncos Under Bowlen

It was sad to learn of the recent passing of Bowlen's, who is easily remembered for the iconic "This one's for John!" saying after handing Elway the Lombardi Trophy in The 1998 Packers-Broncos SuperBowl (The Broncos' first Superbowl victory). After coming so close yet losing so many Super Bowls, The Bowlens were able to capture back to back title wins in the 1997 and 1998 seasons. Much later, John Elway and Ellis would recapture the magic in the 2015 season, with an aging Peyton Manning leading a legendary defense to an easy title against the Carolina Panthers in SuperBowl 50.

OAKLAND RAIDERS OWNER MARK DAVIS

Davis was born in Charleston, South Carolina to Al and Carol Davis. He was named after Mark W. Clark, a U.S. Army General. Davis is a graduate of California State University, Chico. Prior to joining the team, Davis was engaged in the Raiders' retail company where he helped create the Raider Image apparel of the organization. He also spent time developing the muff-style hand warmer for football in the Raiders machinery department. In 1980, Davis represented Raiders player Cliff Branch in contract negotiations with the team which resulted in a deal that included an annuity (still active) and got Mark kicked out of his father's house for being too close to the players. He later lived with Branch when the squad relocated to Los Angeles.

Davis inherited the team after the death of his dad, Al Davis, in 2011. Davis and his wife, Carol, own a 47 percent share of the Raiders, which is contractually structured to offer them controlled ownership. Davis has day-to-day control of the team. Davis acquired control of the team towards the end of the Raiders lease with the O.co Coliseum, a facility that dates back to 1965 and has numerous problems owing to its era. It is also the only stadium which still houses an NFL and an MLB team at the same time.

Davis recently took over the task of setting up a new stadium for the Raiders, a problem his Father Al could never fix in his tenure as owner. He originally indicated a willingness to keep the Raiders in the immediate region in Oakland (preferably on the Coliseum site). Because of the absence of a stadium deal, Davis started to interact with representatives in other cities such as Los Angeles, California, San Antonio, Texas, and finally, Las Vegas, Nevada. At the end of February 2015, Davis announced that the Raiders would establish a joint stadium in Carson, California, with Dean Spanos and the San Diego Chargers. Although the Chargers have historically been inter-divisional rivals, he acknowledged that Spanos was in a comparable situation with San Diego town authorities and that their collaboration could speed up the process of resolving the stadium problem for both franchises.

The Los Angeles Times reported that the relocation of the team could result in the franchise being worth 150% of its present value. The Raiders were seen as a stretch candidate at the time to move to Las Vegas. Napoleon McCallum, former Raiders player and present executive of Las Vegas Sands, set up the meeting. Davis and McCallum, along with then UNLV chairman Don Snyder and Bo Bernhard, the International Gaming Institute's executive director, were present. The meeting would not be known until two years later. On April 23, 2015, a fresh proposal was published for the Carson stadium outlining several personalized touches for shared tenants. These include stadium seats changing from navy blue to black depending on which team homefield, as well as a 120-foot tower on the competition that would serve as a monument for the late Al Davis.

Until after the Carson vote, Davis was also actively working towards a resolution in Oakland. In an interview, he said, "we're trying all we can to get something done in Oakland right on the exact same site we're on right now." The Oakland stadium proposal called for a smaller 55,000-seat stadium at the current site, with space for commercial development and renovations. He was originally working with Sheldon Adelson to get a Las Vegas stadium.

He also toured the University of Nevada, Las Vegas (UNLV) during Davis' conference with Adelson, which included a group of university president Len Jessup, former university president Donald Snyder, Steve Wynn, and former Ultimate Fighting Championship (UFC) owner Lorenzo Fertitta. The stadium is being suggested to replace Sam Boyd Stadium and would be the home of both the Raiders and the UNLV Rebels Football College program. A relocation to Las Vegas would be a long-term proposition as there are no other professional-caliber stadiums in Nevada and Sam Boyd Stadium is undersized for the NFL. Raiders representatives were also in Las Vegas for a prospective new home to tour sites in the valley; they were also on the suggested stadium's 42-acre site to ask questions about the site.

Interviewed by San Jose Mercury News sports columnist Tim Kawakami, Davis said the city as a destination was exciting and that he had an "excellent" visit. Davis also said Las Vegas was a global city and that "it's absolutely an NFL city," as well as saying that "the Raider brand would do well" and "I think Las Vegas is slowly coming along." On March 21, 2016, when asked about Las Vegas, Davis said," I think the Raiders like the Las Vegas plan, and it's a very intriguing and exciting plan", referring to the Las Vegas stadium plan. Davis also met with Governor Brian Sandoval of Nevada on the plan for the stadium. Davis visited Sam Boyd Stadium on April 1, 2016 to assess whether UNLV could serve as the team's temporary home and was with UNLV football coach Tony Sanchez, athletic director Tina Kunzer-Murphy, advisor Don Snyder and college president Len Jessup to investigate further the option of the Raiders relocating to Las Vegas.

On April 28, 2016, Davis said he wished to relocate the Raiders to Las Vegas and promised $500 million to build a suggested $2.4 billion domed stadium: "Together we can transform the Silver State into a silver and black state," Davis said. At a media conference at UNLV's Stan Fulton Building, Davis also said that the club had "committed itself to Las Vegas at this stage in time" On August 11, 2016, Raiders officials met with officials from Northern Nevada about the possibility of Reno being the site of a new training camp / practice facility and toured several sites including the University of Nevada, Reno, high schools in the Reno area and sports complexes. On August 25, 2016, the Raiders filed a trademark application for "Las Vegas Raiders" on the same day of the announcement of a new stadium.

In his short ownership of the Raiders, Davis focused on the business aspects of the team while leaving football in the hands of General Manager Reggie McKenzie. This type of leadership contrasts sharply with his dad, who was well recognized in professional sports as one of the most hands-on managers. In 1966, after returning from a brief stint as AFL chairman, Al Davis became general manager of the Raiders, a position he held after becoming main owner in 1972. He exercised close control over business and football matters until his death.

Davis fired the Raiders Public Relations Director in 2013 because of a Sports Illustrated article that criticized Davis' dad. Davis stated that the replacement of the director needed to understand the importance of his father's legacy and actively protect it. Davis spoke publicly on the issue of domestic violence in the NFL following the arrest of San Francisco 49ers defensive linemen Ray McDonald on 31 August 2014. Davis disagreed with Jed York's decision to keep McDonald on the active roster. In March 2015, Davis again went public with the problem of domestic violence, shutting down rumors that the Raiders began negotiations with Lineman Greg Hardy, who was convicted on charges of domestic abuse previously that year. Traditionally, the Raiders' organization has been vocal about domestic violence problems with direct participation with the Tracey Biletnikoff Foundation established by Hall of Famer Fred Biletnikoff.

Davis has spoken out publicly on the controversial National Anthem protests in the NFL where players kneel during the playing of the pre-game National Anthem to protest social injustice and police brutality on African Americans. Davis initially preferred his players to stand but after President Donald Trump's remarks calling protesting players "Sons of Bitches" and saying they should be fired for kneeling, Davis said he altered his position in a public declaration the following weekend. He stated that "I met Derek Carr and Khalil Mack about a year before our Tennessee match to ask for their approval to have Tommie Smith light the torch for my father", "I clarified to them that I was asking for their approval because I had earlier told them that I would prefer not to protest while in Raiders uniform. And should they have something to say once their uniform is off, I might go up there with them. But over the last year, Davis continued "the streets got warm and there was a lot of static in the air and fuel was added to the fire lately. I can no longer ask our squad not to say anything while they're in a Raider uniform. The only thing I can ask them to do is to do it with class. Do this with pride. Not only do we have to inform individuals that something is wrong, we have to come up with responses. This is the task facing us as Americans and as human beings."

In May 2018, Davis abstained from an NFL owner's resolution on anthem protests calling for players to stand or remain in the locker room until after the anthem is performed or facing a fine for standing, locking arms or lifting their fists. Davis abstained along with San Francisco 49ers owner Jed York after talking to the other owners about social justice issues.

Davis says he is a food connoisseur and said his favorite restaurants include Dan Tana's in Los Angeles, California, Joe's Stone Crab in Miami Beach, Florida, and P.F. Chang's. Davis is renowned for his signature bowl haircut and for riding a 1997 Dodge Caravan SE equipped with a Mark III bubble-top conversion kit as well as a roof-mounted VHS player. Davis donated $10,000 to the Gridiron PAC between 2016 and 2017.

The Raiders under Davis

Year after year for almost all of the current century, the raiders have been awful. Davis is certainly one of the more "Clown Owners" in perception but after reading over his biography further, it seems he could be a bit misunderstood. The Las Vegas deal is solid, and will open a new exciting market and universal fanbase for the Raiders. Overall however, the GM and coaching staff have made very questionable personnel decisions that have made them the laughingstock of the NFL. It remains to be seen in 2019 and beyond if Coach Jon Gruden and Davis can improve the team from the basement dwellers that they are.

KANSAS CITY CHIEFS OWNER CLARK HUNT

Clark Hunt (born February 19, 1965) is part owner, chairman and CEO of the Kansas City Chiefs of the National Football League and a founding investor-owner in Major League Soccer. Hunt also serves as chairman of the Hunt Sports Group, where he oversees the activities of FC Dallas and, formerly, the MLS Columbus crew. He is the son of Lamar Hunt and the grandson of oil tycoon H.L. Hunt. Following the death of his father in 2006, Hunt and his siblings co-inherited ownership of the Chiefs. As the team's CEO and public face of the ownership group, he represents the Chiefs at all owners meetings and handles the day-to-day operations of the team.

Hunt was born on February 19, 1965. He is the son of Lamar Hunt and the grandson of oil tycoon H.L. Hunt. After graduating from St. Mark's School of Texas, he finished first in his class at Southern Methodist University in 1987, where he was a captain of SMU's nationally ranked soccer team and a two-time Academic All-American. Hunt earned a degree in Business Administration with a concentration in Finance. He was a two-time recipient of the greatest academic honor of the university, the Provost Award for Outstanding Scholar.

One of the driving forces behind the creation of Major League Soccer, Hunt helped his father run the Kansas City Wizards until the team was sold in 2006. Hunt remains a member of the league's board of governors and owns the MLS club FC Dallas. He previously owned the Columbus Crew until 2013.

Hunt was named chairman of the Kansas City Chiefs in 2005. Following the death of his father in 2006, he, his sister, and two brothers inherited ownership of the Chiefs. However, Hunt serves as the operating head of the franchise; he represents the Chiefs at owner's meetings and has the final say on personnel changes.

After the Chiefs' loss to the New York Jets in the 2007 season finale, Chiefs general manager Carl Peterson announced that both he and head coach Herm Edwards would return to the Chiefs in 2008. However, Hunt declined to immediately comment on Peterson's status. Hunt spoke out weeks later and stated that the Chiefs were his "No. 1 priority" and that "to have the best chance of success in 2008, having Carl here makes a lot of sense." Hunt wanted to avoid having a new general manager come in with a new head coach, and starting from scratch again. However on December 15, Hunt announced the firing of Peterson from his position as General Manager, President, and CEO of the franchise effective the end of the season. Prior to the decision, the Chiefs had a combined record of 9–24 under Hunt's leadership since December 23, 2006.

The official press release indicated that Peterson had resigned, but Hunt had said the discussion had been continuous throughout the season. Hunt said his choice to relieve Peterson of responsibilities was not based on what occurred the day before when the Chiefs lost an 11-point lead in the final 73 seconds and were beaten 22–21 by San Diego, reducing their record to 2–12 in the season. On January 23 the Chiefs fired head coach Herman Edwards, and Todd Haley was hired as his replacement on

February 6. In Later Chief seasons (2011-2013) Hunt fired Todd Haley on December 12, 2011, after the Chiefs had compiled a 5–8 record during the 2011 NFL season. Haley was replaced by defensive coordinator Romeo Crennel. Crennel finished his stint as interim head coach with a 2–1 record, including a win over the previously-undefeated, and defending Super Bowl Champions (2011 Green Bay Packers season).

On January 9, 2012, Hunt named Crennel the team's permanent head coach. The return of star players Jamaal Charles and Eric Berry led many to believe that the Chiefs would contend for a playoff spot. Instead, the Chiefs were historically bad through the first seven games of the season, failing to lead a game during regulation (worst since 1940), and holding a tie at the end of only two of twenty-eight possible quarters. Through seven games, the Chiefs were on pace to break the 1965 Pittsburgh Steelers record for worst turnover ratio by 11 turnovers. On October 28, 2012, the Chiefs lost to rival Oakland Raiders for the sixth consecutive time at home.

To date, the only public comment Hunt has made during the season has been in defense of Chiefs fans, who were accused by new right tackle Eric Winston of cheering Matt Cassell's head injury during a game on October 7, 2012. Local and national media outlets have referred to the 1-6 Chiefs' start as "rock bottom" and "competing against history". On January 4, 2013, Kansas City Chiefs officially hired Andy Reid to be the next head coach. The rest is history, as the Chiefs under Reid have been completely revitalized and have seen their offense rise to the most dangerous in the entire league. Unfortunately for the Chiefs, even though they saw a record breaking 2018 season with Patrick Mahoes at the QB helm, the team still fell short in a dramatic loss to the New England Patriots in the AFC Championship.

Hunt is married to Tavia Shackles, a former Miss Missouri Teen USA and Miss Kansas USA. The couple have three children.

The Chiefs Under Hunt

Most has already been covered in the paragraphs above. Hunt has seen some awful stretches as owner of the Chiefs but since the Andy reid hiring the Chiefs have seen a major uptick in production. Andy Reid is not necessarily notorious for playoff success though, and get over the final hump may seem attainable in the next few years but nothing is guaranteed in the NFL. Still having a solid offensive core manned by Patrick Mahomes likely ensures the Chiefs win their division or make the playoffs frequently over the next decade.

LOS ANGELES CHARGERS OWNER DEAN SPANOS

Dean Alexander Spanos (born May 26, 1950) is the owner and chairman of the Los Angeles Chargers franchise and on the Board for the National Football League (NFL). He is the son of Alex Spanos, who bought majority interest from the Chargers in 1984. Spanos took over regular activities for the team from his dad in 1994, becoming president and CEO, until Alex transferred activities and Ownership to his children in 2015. After his father's death on October 9, 2018, Spanos took over complete possession of the Chargers.

Spanos was raised in Stockton, California, the son of both Greek ancestry Alex and Faye Spanos. Spanos attended Lincoln High School where he received varsity letters in football and golf and the Lincoln High Hall of Fame Award. He Graduated University of the Pacific in 1972.

Spanos was named team president and chief executive officer of the Chargers in early 1994. Under Spanos' leadership, the Chargers won 113 games between 2004 and 2014, which included five AFC West championships and four playoff game wins. In May 2015, Alex Spanos ceded control of the team to his sons,

John and A.G. He stayed on as chairman with the understanding he would oversee the new stadium process, which resulted in the team playing its home games in the LA Galaxy's StubHub Center, which was not full for several games in 2017. Spanos demanded the San Diego taxpayers finance a new stadium for the Chargers to be built in downtown San Diego. After 15 years of attempting to finance a downtown football stadium, the vote received only 43 percent approval.

In January 2017, Spanos exercised the option to relocate the team to Los Angeles. The move was met with criticism by the San Diego fan base, due to Spanos' lack of effort in attempting to find a stadium solution in San Diego. The team's temporary headquarters was in Costa Mesa under a 10 year lease. The 2017 season was played at the 27,000-seat Dignity Health Sports Park (known as StubHub Center until 2019) and the Chargers are scheduled to play at Los Angeles Stadium at Hollywood Park along with the Los Angeles Rams in 2020.

In 2000, the family launched Chargers Champions through the Community Foundation to support local schools. In 2011 Spanos held a fundraiser for Rick Perry at a private event at Sacramento. In 2014, the Spanos' donated $500,000 to the University of California, San Diego for the Alex G. Spanos Athletic Performance Center. The donation brought their total support to UCSD to $1.6 million. He also led the Chargers to partner with the Susan G. Komen Foundation in San Diego in honor of his wife Susie, who is a breast cancer survivor. During his tenure with the Chargers, Spanos created The Chargers Champions All-Star Gala to recognize high school students and educators in the San Diego area. After Hurricane Harvey in 2017, Spanos and the Chargers donated $500,000 to hurricane relief.]

In 2016, Spanos ranked number 21 on the USA Today list of

the 100 most important people in the NFL. He was an honoree at the American Hellenic Council's (AHC) Annual Awards Gala, which recognizes individuals from the Greek-American community. He was appointed to the board of the John F. Kennedy Center for the Performing Arts in Washington, D.C. by President George W. Bush in 2006. Spanos received the 2005 Distinguished American Award from the San Diego Chapter of the National Football Foundation. He was also awarded the 2004 Jose A. Cota Award for philanthropy and the Chargers support of law enforcement. In 2002, Spanos was awarded the Ellis Island Medal of Honor, 16 years after his father received the award. He also was inducted into the DeMolay International Alumni Hall of Fame.

The Chargers Under Spanos

The decision to relocate to Los Angeles will remain controversial, but business is business for the Chargers. Excellent every year, the team compiles an annual superior offense and defense but succumbs to better competition in the playoffs. Their best shots were in the middle 00's (2006 and 2007 season) But fell controversially to the New England Patriots each time. With an aging QB (Rivers) The Chargers still have a decent shot of winning their division, but their longevity and "win now" window is quickly closing.

NFC

NFC EAST

COWBOYS OWNER JERRY JONES

Jerral Wayne Jones (born October 13, 1942) is an American billionaire businessman, best known for being the owner of the National Football League (NFL)'s Dallas Cowboys since 1989.

Jones was born in Los Angeles, California. His family moved to North Little Rock, Arkansas in 1945. Jones' Father J.W. "Pat" Jones (1920–1997) and mother Armenita Pearl Clark Jones (1922–2012) married in 1941. They owned two branches of Pat's SuperMarket in the Rose City neighborhood of North Little Rock. Jones was a running back at North Little Rock High School, graduating in 1960. After his graduation, his parents moved to Springfield, Missouri, where Pat was president and chairman of Modern Security Life Insurance Co. The company, which an advertisement billed as a "one in a million" company, saw its assets increase from $440,299.76 in its first statement in 1961 to $6,230,607 in 1965. After graduating from the University of Arkansas, Jerral W. Jones was listed as an executive vice president.

With the success of the company the couple bought the 5,500 acre Buena Vista Ranch East of Springfield in Rogersville, Missouri in the Ozark Mountains. In 1971, after selling the insurance company, the couple carved out 400 acres of their ranch to start Buena Vista Animal Paradise, where tourists would visit exotic animals (now Wild Animal Safari in Strafford, Missouri, just south of Interstate 44).

Jerry Jones attended the University of Arkansas, where he was a member of the Kappa Sigma fraternity. He was also a co-captain of the 1964 National Championship football team. He was an all-Southwest Conference offensive lineman for College Football Hall of Fame coach Frank Broyles and a teammate of college football and NFL coach Jimmy Johnson, whom Jones hired as his first head coach after purchasing the Cowboys. Other notable teammates were Glen Ray Hines, a consensus All-American offensive tackle; Ken Hatfield, who went on to coach several major programs including Arkansas; Jim Lindsey; future Outland Trophy winner Lloyd Phillips; and College Football Hall of Fame linebacker Ronnie Caveness. Several future head coaches were assistant coaches for Broyles on the Razorbacks' staff during Jones's college career in Fayetteville, including three more members of the College Football Hall of Fame: Hayden Fry (University of Iowa); Johnny Majors (Iowa State University, University of Pittsburgh and University of Tennessee), and Barry Switzer (University of Oklahoma, and later head coach of the Cowboys under Jones). Jones is one of a very small number of NFL owners who had a significant level of success as a football player, Jerry Richardson of the Carolina Panthers being another.

According to an interview with Jones on HBO, after graduating from college in 1965, he borrowed a million dollars from Jimmy Hoffa's Teamsters union to open up a string of Shakey's Pizza Parlor restaurants in Missouri. When that venture failed, Jones was given a job at his father's insurance company Modern Security Life of Springfield, Missouri. He received his Master's degree in business in 1970. After several other unsuccessful business ventures (including an attempt, again using Teamsters money, to purchase the American Football League's San Diego Chargers in 1967), he began an oil and gas exploration business in Arkansas, Jones Oil and Land Lease, which became successful. His privately held company currently does natural resource prospecting. In 2008, Jones formed a partnership with Yankee Global Enterprises to create Legends Hospitality, a food, beverage, merchandise, retail and stadium operations corporation serving entertainment venues.

On February 25, 1989, Jones purchased the Cowboys from H.R. "Bum" Bright for $140 million. Soon after the purchase, he fired longtime coach Tom Landry, to that point the only coach in the team's history, in favor of his old teammate at Arkansas, Jimmy Johnson. A few months later, he fired longtime general manager Tex Schramm, and assumed complete control over football matters. After a slow start under Jones and Johnson (the first season under Jones, a 1–15 finish, remains second only to the team's inaugural season in terms of futility), Jones quickly built a team that is often reckoned to be the best NFL franchise of the 1990s. The Cowboys won Super Bowl XXVII in the 1992 season, as well as Super Bowl XXVIII the following year in the 1993 season. Johnson then departed and was replaced by Barry Switzer, who also went on to win Super Bowl XXX in the 1995 season. At the time of the sale, the financially troubled Bright claimed to be losing $1 million per month on the franchise. During Jones' tenure, the Cowboys have appreciated in value to an estimated $4.2 billion, turning their owner into a billionaire in the process. Much of the league's financial success since 1989 has been credited to Jones himself. In particular, he was decisive in securing Fox as the NFC's primary broadcaster at a time when the traditional "Big Three" networks were trying to convince the league into accepting a rollback in television rights fees. Increased television revenues have played a decisive role in securing the NFL's place as the world's richest sports league, with revenues of well over $10 billion per season. The 2018 NFL season is Jones' 30th as Cowboys owner; more than the number of seasons as the combined tenures of his predecessors.

In an online poll from October 8, 2003, Jones was named the least favorite sports personality by Sports Illustrated, in three states (Virginia, Delaware and Texas). Jones is often vilified by fans who remain bitter at his unceremonious firing of long-time Cowboys personnel who were fan-favorites, head coach Tom Landry and general manager Tex Schramm, even though the Cowboys had been doing poorly in the last few seasons before Jones became the team owner. Jones stated he did not give consideration to retaining Landry for even a season, as he said he would not have purchased the team unless he could hire Johnson as coach. Jones also did not discuss the matter beforehand with Landry before announcing the decision. This was denounced by football fans and media as totally lacking in class and respect, as pride and tradition were part of the Cowboys where great performance and loyal service were expected to be rewarded. Since the dismissal, Jones has indicated he regrets the process of Landry's firing and his role in it. It would later emerge that Jones' predecessor Bright had been dissatisfied with Landry for years and had even offered to relieve Jones of the inevitable criticism by dismissing the longtime coach himself prior to selling the team. Some of the fan criticism is due to Jones' high visibility and involvement as the "face of the team", a marked contrast to original owner Clint Murchison Jr.

Jones' prominent role has led to fans expressing their displeasure with him and the lack of success of the franchise, with particular criticism focusing on Jones' insistence on serving as his own general manager. There was particular criticism of Jones over his conflict with head coach Jimmy Johnson, as Jones who was general manager "wanted Cowboys fans to know he had helped build those Super Bowl-winning teams", while "Johnson insisted that he made all of the personnel moves" since he had the final say in football matters and refused to relinquish this power; consequently Jones ousted Johnson after the 1993 season despite winning two consecutive Super Bowls and has refused to induct Johnson into the Cowboys Ring of Honor. Jones also initially promised head coach Bill Parcells complete control over football matters, however their relationship broke down after Jones signed controversial wide receiver Terrell Owens. Parcell's successor as Cowboys head coach, Wade Phillips, had complained to friends about being "undermined and second-guessed, repeatedly" by Jones. Jones is one of two owners in the league (the other being Cincinnati's Mike Brown) who have either the title or powers of general manager.

Over the years of Jones's tenure, Cowboys fans have organized a number of grassroots efforts aimed at displacing Jones from his position. Jones is the subject of the 2008 book Playing to Win by David Magee. In the book, Jones admitted he handled the firing of Landry poorly and accepted some blame for the disintegration of his relationship with Landry's successor, Jimmy Johnson. Jones became involved in the St. Louis Rams move back to Los Angeles with Stan Kroenke in 2016. He was instrumental in brokering a deal between Kroenke, San Diego Chargers owner Dean Spanos, and Oakland Raiders owner Mark Davis to ensure that Kroenke's Inglewood Stadium plan passed, which it did, via a 30-2 owners vote in favor. Jones' support and role in the negotiations has been criticized by some fans and sports media in St. Louis.

Jones has also been notorious for racking up fines during his time in the NFL. Jones was fined $25,000 by the NFL for publicly criticizing referee Ed Hochuli after Hochuli made a controversial call in a game between the San Diego Chargers and the Denver Broncos on September 14, 2008. Comments were published to the media as well as to his radio show, stating that Hochuli was one of the most criticized NFL officials. This was the NFL's first fine for Jones. Jones was fined $100,000 in 2009 for breaking a gag order on labor problems, commenting that revenue sharing was "on its way out." Commissioner Roger Goodell issued a gag order for all managers and team managers to discuss any aspect of the pending labor problems. Sources said that Jones "crossed the line," drawing a "six-figure" fine, as the commissioner distributed a memo to all 32 owners, along with a reminder that the gag order remains in effect. Jones was the inspiration in the 1998 movie BASEketball for the character Baxter Cain (Robert Vaughn), owner of the Dallas Felons. In the 1998 made-for-television reunion film Dallas: War of the Ewings, he had a short cameo appearance like himself.

Jones also appeared as himself in a 1996 episode of the Coach TV show and in a 2007 Diet Pepsi MAX TV commercial, which also featured Cowboys head coach Wade Phillips and Quarterback Tony Romo.

He appeared as himself in the seventh season of the HBO Entourage series in 2010, in an episode of Dallas ' TNT incarnation entitled "Truth and Consequences," aired on July 4, 2012, in a series of commercials for ESPN's Monday Night Football season 2012, and in The League's season 4 premiere. In 2013, Jones narrated a documentary film about former teammate and business partner Jim Lindsey. Jones also appears in a 2013 Pepsi commercial, walking into an elevator filled with three men wearing New York Giants clothes who look at him with dissatisfaction. He was parodied on the first episode, "Go Fund Yourself," of South Park's eighteenth season, along with several other NFL teams owing to him. In one scene, Jones is portrayed as having large, bulging chameleon-like eyes, as the head of a young woman emerges from his lap.

The Cowboys under Jones

Credit is due for being one of the longest tenured owners in the league as well as the legendary 90's Cowboys Dynasty. But what have the Cowboys done since. With the 90's long in the rear view mirror, the Cowboys continue to be a team that draws hype and attention yet never delivers. A Decade ago, having attained the #1 seed in the NFC, they nonetheless choked at the hands of the New York Giants, and have failed in multiple playoff appearances. They haven't even reached the NFC Championship since the 1995 season, a baffling statement for such a hyped team.

Unlike other teams reviewed here, this one does in fact fall squarely on the shoulders on the owner. Just like the next owner to be reviewed, Jones takes far too heavy of a handed approach, functioning as his own GM and in turn making costly personnel decisions and potentially ruining morale. In the recent Cowboys version of Hard Knocks, Jones comes across as a good leader, and fair when dealing with his staff and players. Yet, the lack of success of a good but never great team of nearly 30 years can be traced back to him.

REDSKINS OWNER DANIEL SNYDER

Daniel Marc Snyder (born 23 November 1964) is an American businessman who is the majority owner of the American football team of Washington Redskins, founder of Snyder Communications and main investor of Red Zebra Broadcasting, home to Redskins Radio ESPN.

Snyder was born on 23 November 1964 in Maryland. He moved to Henley-on-Thames, a tiny city near London, at the age of 12, where he attended private school. He returned to the United States at the age of 14 and lived in Queens, New York with his grandma. He moved back to Maryland a year later and graduated from Charles W. Woodward High School in Rockville, Maryland. His first work was at B. Dalton's White Flint Mall bookstore. At the age of 17, Snyder had his first business failure when he partnered with his dad to sell bus-trip packages to Washington Capitals fans to see their hockey team playing in Philadelphia. By the age of 20, he had dropped out of the University of Maryland, College Park and ran his own business, leasing jets to fly College Spring Breakers to exotic destinations. Snyder claims to have cleared US$1 million running the business out of his parents' bedroom with a friend and several telephone lines.

Snyder courted real estate entrepreneur Mortimer Zuckerman, whose US News & World Report was also interested in the college market and who agreed to finance his push to publish Campus USA, a magazine for college students. Zuckerman and Fred Drasner, co-publisher of Zuckerman's New York Daily News, invested $3 million in Campus USA. The venture did not generate enough paid advertising and was forced to close after two years.

In 1989, Snyder and his sister Michele established a wallboard advertising company with seed money from his dad, who took a second mortgage on his estate in England, and his sister, who maxed out their credit cards at $35,000. They focused on wallboards in doctor's offices (where there was a captive audience) and universities. They married the advertisement with the distribution of product samples such as soaps and medicine packages — to distinguish themselves from their competitors. The firm was named Snyder Communications LP. The business was a wonderful success, and Snyder and his sister grew the business organically and through acquisitions and extended their business to cover all elements of outsourced industry. Revenues from Snyder Communications rose from $2.7 million in 1991 to $4.1 million in 1992 and $9 million in 1993. Proprietary product sampling was launched in 1992 through their personal day care center network. In September 1996, Daniel Snyder became the youngest ever CEO of a New York Stock Exchange listed company at the age of 32. By 1998, the firm had more than 12,000 staff and an annual revenue of $1 billion. In April 2000, Snyder Communications was sold to the French advertising and marketing services group Havas in an all-stock transaction worth more than $2 billion, the biggest transaction in the advertising / market industry's history. Snyder's private share of the proceeds was estimated to be US $300 million. In May 1999, Snyder purchased Redskins and Jack Kent Cooke Stadium (now FedEx Field) for $800 million following the death of former owner Jack Kent Cooke. At that moment, it was the most costly transaction in the history of professional sports.

Under Snyder, the team has had a losing record (139-180-1 through the end of the 2018 season) since he purchased the Redskins. They also went through eight head coaches in 17 seasons. Several Washington newspaper articles criticized Snyder in October 2009, claiming that his managerial style was partially attributable to the on-field fighting of the Redskins. Although unsuccessful year after year, criticism of Snyder and his General Manager, Vinny Cerrato, escalated after a 3-7 beginning to the 2009 Washington Redskins season. Fans and football analysts have criticized the revolving door of Redskins head coaches employed since Snyder purchased the team, as well as Snyder and Cerrato's pattern of employing costly free agents and trading off draft picks for older players instead of recruiting young talent through the NFL draft.

The Redskins sued season ticket holders under Snyder who were unable to pay during the U.S. recession of 2008–2009. Snyder did so despite his statement that there are more than 200,000 individuals on the waiting list for a season ticket. Snyder banned all signs from FedEx Field partly through the 2009 season, leading to further fan discontent. The ban was lifted soon thereafter. Writing in Forbes magazine, Monte Burke says that Snyder's complete stubbornness about changing the potentially racist Washington Redskins team name has made the name controversy worse than it needs to be. The ongoing controversy seems to have died down recently but appears to be a terminal battle.

Snyder has also bristled the tradition Redskin fan, no doubt nostalgic about the 80's and 90's when the team was a 3 time Super Bowl Champion. One fan describes: "Too much hoopla exists… Fireworks. Heavy music. It is no longer about the game. In an artificial manner, they try to create enthusiasm. It's just a diversion. Redskins fans are faithful and loud—they can do it on their own."

91

Threatening a lawsuit in January 2011, Snyder requested that Washington City Paper's sports writer Dave McKenna be fired, who had written a long article for the alternative journal" The Cranky Redskins Fan's Guide to Dan Snyder". McKenna had been needling Snyder for years in his columns, and the front-page of the article had a defaced picture of Snyder with Devil's Horns and a scraggly beard, which incensed Snyder who felt the picture was antisemitic. Other sportswriters have come out in support of McKenna. In a statement released by the Simon Wiesenthal Center, while acknowledging that public figures are fair game for criticism, said the artwork used by the City Paper was reminiscent of "virulent anti-Semitism going back to the Middle Ages" and urged the City Paper issue an apology. Mike Madden of the City Paper issued a statement saying they take accusations of antisemitism very seriously and said the artwork was meant to "resemble the type of scribbling that teenagers everywhere have been using to deface photos" and the cover art was not an antisemitic caricature. Snyder made good on his threat, and on February 2, 2011 filed suit against the City Paper. Two months later McKenna was also added to the suit as a defendant. In September 2011 however, Snyder dropped the lawsuit against both parties.

Snyder owned expansion rights to an Arena Football League team for the Washington, D.C. market before the 2009 demise of the original league. He purchased the rights to the team for $4 million in 1999. The team was going to be called the Washington Warriors and play their games at the Comcast Center in 2003 but the team never got off the ground. In 2005, he bought 12% of stock of amusement park operator Six Flags through his private equity company called RedZone Capital. He later gained control of the board placing his friend and ESPN executive Mark Shapiro as CEO and himself as chairman. In April 2009, the New York Stock Exchange delisted Six Flags' stock as it had fallen below the minimal required market capitalization. In June 2009, Six Flags announced that they were delaying a $15 million debt payment and two weeks later, Six Flags filed for Chapter 11 bankruptcy protection. As part of the reorganization, 92% of the company ended up in the hands of their lenders and Dan Snyder and Mark Shapiro were removed from their positions. Snyder lost his entire investment. In July 2006, Snyder's Red Zebra Broadcasting launched a trio of sports radio stations in his home market of Washington, D.C. known as Triple X ESPN Radio but, due to Snyder's perceived heavy-handedness, some referred to him as 'Dan Jazeera'. He purchased other radio stations in the mid-Atlantic region, and intends to broadcast coverage of Washington Redskins games on all of his stations.

In July 2006, Snyder and other investors signed a deal to provide financing to the production company run by Tom Cruise and his partner, Paula Wagner. This came one week after Paramount Pictures severed its ties with Cruise and Wagner. Snyder is credited as an executive producer for the 2008 movie Valkyrie, which stars Cruise. In February 2007, it was announced that Snyder's private equity firm Red Zone Capital Management would purchase Johnny Rockets, the 1950s-themed diner chain. RedZone Capital Management sold the company to Sun Capital Partners in 2013. On June 19, 2007, Snyder purchased Dick Clark Productions for $175 million. In 2012, Dick Clark Productions was sold to a group including investment firm Guggenheim Partners.

He contributed $1 million to help the victims of the September 11 attacks; he donated $600,000 to help victims of Hurricane Katrina; and he paid the shipping costs for charitable food shipments to aid those affected by the 2004 tsunami in Indonesia and Thailand. His disaster relief efforts continued in 2016 following Hurricane Matthew, dispatching his private plane to provide emergency supplies in the Bahamas and medical supplies to Hospital Bernard Mevs in Port-au-Prince, Haiti. In 2000, Snyder founded the Washington Redskins Charitable Foundation, which is active in the Washington, D.C. area. Snyder has been a long-time supporter of Youth For Tomorrow, an organization founded by former Redskins head coach and Pro Football Hall of Famer Joe Gibbs. In April 2010, the organization presented Snyder with its Distinguished Leader Award.

In 2014, Snyder formed the Washington Redskins Original Americans Foundation to provide opportunities and resources to aid Tribal communities. The foundation was formed to address the challenges in the daily lives of Native Americans. Snyder has also supported the Washington's Children's Hospital, the National Center for Missing and Exploited Children (NCMEC), and other organizations. In May 2014, Snyder and his wife Tanya received the Charles B. Wang International Children's Award from the NCMEC.

In 2004, Snyder brokered a deal with the National Park Service to remove old growth trees from the 200 feet (61 m) of national parkland behind his home to grant him a better view of the Potomac River, on the condition that Snyder would replace the trees with 600 native saplings. Lenn Harley, a real estate broker who was not involved in Snyder's purchase of the estate but was familiar with the area, estimated that the relatively unobstructed view of the river and its surroundings that resulted from Snyder's clearing could add $500,000 to $1 million to his $10 million home's value. The clearcutting was started without approval from Montgomery County, Maryland, and without environmental assessments, as required by law. As a result, Snyder was fined $100 by the Maryland-National Capital Park and Planning Commission in December 2004. Snyder's neighbors also filed complaints regarding his clearcutting of scenic and historic easements behind his home. The NPS ranger that investigated the complaints of Snyder's neighbors and clearcutting along the Potomac was transferred multiple times due to his continued pursuit of the complaints and the Snyder property. Eventually, the NPS ranger filed a whistleblower complaint regarding the Snyder case. Later, the ranger's anonymity as a whistleblower was lost, potentially leading to extreme harassment and a trial of the park ranger, ultimately ending the ranger's career. Snyder has still not replanted the trees and has faced no other consequences aside from his fine.

In 1994, he married Tanya Ivey, a former fashion model from Atlanta. Tanya Snyder is now a national spokesperson for breast cancer awareness. They have three children. In 2005, Snyder was inducted as a member of the Greater Washington Jewish Sports Hall of Fame. Snyder owns a corporate jet, a Bombardier BD-700 Global Express XRS[68] with tail number N904DS and it is hangared at Dulles International Airport. The tail sports a Redskin helmet. On February 1, 2019, the Los Angeles Times featured Mr. Snyder's second yacht, which contains an IMAX theater, in an op-ed titled, "America is falling out of love with billionaires, and it's about time."

The Redskins Under Snyder

It's a harsh take, but out of all the 32 owners in the NFL, Snyder is likely the worst. The team is rife with mediocrity, from frequent coaching changes, bad quarterbacks, embarrassing signings, and a heavy handed owner that gets in the way of his team's success. Since buying the team many years ago, the farthest they have achieved in the postseason was the division round (2005). The team is a perennial loser, and has some of the most boring offensive weapons year in and year out. They are likely not to improve with Snyder as the owner unless he scales back some of his involvement, as his input clearly hasn't worked.

NEW YORK GIANTS OWNERS JON MARA AND STEVE TISCH

John K. Mara, is the chairman, Chief Executive Officer and co-owner of the New York Giants (b. 1 December 1954).

Mara was born in New York City and grew up in the neighboring suburb of White Plains. He is the eldest child of Ann Mara (born Mumm) and son of Giants Wellington Mara. His ancestors include Irish, German and French Canadians.

Mara joined the Giants in 1988, serving as General Counsel and later as Executive Vice President and Chief Operating Officer until his father's death in 2005, when he assumed the chairmanship of the team. Under John Mara and Steve Tisch, the Giants won Super Bowl XLII and Super Bowl XLVI.

Mara's additional job has been on the NFL Competition Committee for 15 years. He is the present chairperson of the Executive Committee of the NFL Management Board. In February 2014, Mara, along with Steve Tisch and Woody Johnson, brought Super Bowl XLVIII to MetLife Stadium. Personal life Mara is his family's third generation to own the Giants. The team was established in 1925 by his grandpa, Tim. In 1959, when Tim died, the sons of Tim, Wellington and Jack (John's uncle), inherited the team. Among the NFL franchises, only the Chicago Bears (ruled by the Halas-McCaskey family since 1921) were in the hands of one family longer than the Giants. He and his wife, Denise W. Mara, had one son, John Jr., and four sisters, Lauren, Courtney, Christine, and Erin. He was also an aunt to the actors Rooney Mara and Kate Mara.

Steve Tisch

Steven Elliot Tisch (born February 14, 1949) is a producer and businessman of American films. He is New York Giants' President, Co-Owner and Executive Vice President, his family-owned NFL team, as well as a producer of film and television. He is the son of Bob Tisch, former co-owner of the Giants.

Tisch was born in Lakewood Township, New Jersey, son of Joan Tisch (born Hyman) and Preston Robert Tisch, a film and television executive who also served as Postmaster General of the United States. He attended Tufts University, during which he began his filmmaking career. During his youth, Tisch created a number of small films with the support of Columbia Pictures. In 1976, he left Columbia and created his first feature film, Outlaw Blues. This was followed up in 1983 by Risky Business, which gave Tom Cruise his first lead role. In 1986, Tisch introduced his own Production Company, The Steve Tisch Company, which has been specializing in tiny screen movies since then. He also produced several critically acclaimed films, including Forrest Gump, American History X, and Snatch.

Tisch received a Best Motion Picture Academy Award and a Golden Globe for Forrest Gump, nominated for 13 Academy

Awards and winning six, and remains one of the highest grossing films in the history of the domestic box office. He is also the only individual ever to have a Golden Globe, an Academy Award, a nomination for the Primetime Emmy Award, and a Super Bowl Ring.

He is presently a partner in Escape Artists, an independently funded movie manufacturing firm based at Sony Pictures Entertainment resulting from a merger between his Steve Tisch Company and his fellow associates Todd Black and Jason Blumenthal's Company. He was awarded Tufts University's Barnum Award for his outstanding job in the media and entertainment fields.

Tisch was appointed Chairman and Executive Vice President of the New York Giants American Football Team in 2005. Tisch received the Vince Lombardi Trophy twice, when the Giants won Super Bowl XLII and again when they won Super Bowl XLVI.

The Giants under Mara and Tisch

Although relatively ineffective over the last few seasons, the Giants and their owners remain the class of the NFL. The Franchise has had more than its healthy share of Championship Success, and represents New York in a big way.

PHILADELPHIA EAGLES OWNER JEFFREY LURIE

Jeffrey Robert Lurie (born September 8, 1951) is an American film producer and businessman and owner of the National Football League (NFL) Philadelphia Eagles.

Lurie was born to a Jewish family in Boston, MA. His grandfather, Philip Smith, established the General Cinema movie theater chain, one of America's biggest drive-in cinema operators. His uncle is Richard A. Smith. He's got two brothers: Peter and Cathy. His father died at the age of 44 on April 14, 1961, when he was the age of nine.

General Cinema started to acquire bottling franchises in the late 1960s, including a bottling operation by Pepsi. Over the years, General Cinema has developed into Harcourt General Inc., a $3.7 billion conglomerate with 23,700 staff globally based in Chestnut Hill, Massachusetts. It was the fourth biggest chain of film theatres in the nation in its heyday, owning several publication houses, three insurance companies and a major worldwide consulting company. Carter Hawley Hale was purchased in 1984, which at the moment was the United States' fifth biggest apparel retailer, including Bergdorf Goodman and Neiman-Marcus.

Lurie got a B.A. From Clark University, a Master of Psychology degree from Boston University, and a PhD in Social Policy from Brandeis University, where he wrote his thesis on depicting females in Hollywood films. He was born to Jewish parents but spent his adult life as a non-practicing Jew. Lurie served as an adjunct professor of social policy at Boston University before joining the company.

He left the University in 1983 to join General Cinema Corporation. As a liaison between General Cinema Corporation and the Hollywood manufacturing community, he worked as an executive in the business. He was also an adviser to the National Film Buying Office at The General Cinema.

He then established Chestnut Hill Productions in 1985, producing a series of Hollywood films and television shows. They Included 1988 Sweet Hearts Dance, 1990's I Love You To Death V.I. Warshawski (producer), The Blind Side (TV film) (executive producer) 1994 State of emergency (TV film) (executive producer) 1996 Malibu Shores (TV series) (co-producer) 10 episodes 1996 Foxfire (producer), Sergio (documentary) (executive producer) 2010 Inside Job (documentary) (executive producer)

As a fan of all Boston sports teams, Lurie went to matches and slept listening to the Boston Red Sox on his transistor radio. Since the New England Patriots franchise started in 1960, the year the American Football League was established, the Luries had been season ticket holders. Gino Cappelletti, Houston Ansine and Babe Parilli were cheered by Lurie. Lurie attempted to buy the New England Patriots in 1993, but he fell $150 million from the bid when his uncle Richard Smith nixed the financial-based purchase.

Lurie's name had also emerged in sales discussions about the

Los Angeles Rams, and he was a prospective investor in a bid with Robert Tisch for a Baltimore expansion team, who eventually purchased 50% of the New York Giants. Smith agreed to allow his nephew to purchase the Philadelphia Eagles five months later. Lurie approached the then owner of the Eagles, Norman Braman. Lurie paid $195 million to Braman for the Philadelphia Eagles on May 6, 1994. Lurie and his wife, Nancy Lurie Marks of Chestnut Hill, Massachusetts borrowed $190 million from the Bank of Boston to purchase the Eagles. To support the loan from the Bank of Boston, Lurie put up millions of dollars worth of private inventory in Harcourt General and GC Companies Inc. as equity capital. Additionally, he and his mother pledged their stock in the family trust as collateral so Lurie could borrow the rest. The club is now estimated at $2.65 billion, as Forbes ranked 10th in the NFL in terms of team value in 2017.

On February 4, 2018, the Eagles beat the Patriots and won Super Bowl LII with a score of 41–33, giving Lurie his first title as Eagles owner. The win evened the score with New England, as a 24-21 loss to the Patriots in Super Bowl XXXIX was the only other appearance of the Lurie era Super Bowl.

Lurie had originally been married for the first time and then got divorced. They had two kids: a son Julian and a daughter Milena. In 2012, the couple announced their divorce; the divorce was completed in August 2012. As part of the divorce settlement, she got a "significant" stake in the Philadelphia Eagles. He married Tina Lai on May 4, 2013.

The Eagles Under Lurie

Another great owner, The Eagles struggled with mediocrity for the first few years under Lurie but since 2001 have been a major powerhouse in the NFC East and the NFL at large. Always in contention, the Eagles are now better than ever with scouting talent, particularly dynamic offensive playmakers. They are poised for another run in 2019.

NFC NORTH

CHICAGO BEARS OWNER VIRGINIA HALAS MCCASKEY

Virginia Halas McCaskey (born January 5, 1923) is the National Football League's main owner of the Chicago Bears. She is the eldest child of former Bears coach and owner George Halas, who left the team to his daughter after his death in 1983, and Minnie Bushing Halas. After the death of Buffalo Bills owner Ralph Wilson in March 2014, she became the oldest NFL owner. Her official title within the Bears organisation is secretary of the board of directors.

The brother of McCaskey, George "Mugs" Halas Jr., was the obvious heir to the franchise, but unexpectedly he died of a heart attack in 1979. As a consequence, when her dad died, McCaskey inherited an incredible team nucleus and was the owner when the Bears won Super Bowl XX. Nevertheless, the team struggled in the 1990s and since 1999 she has been a very hands-off owner. Her son Michael McCaskey was team president from 1983 to 1999 and was board chairman until May 6, 2011, when his brother George McCaskey assumed the positive. Although McCaskey never had any formal share of ownership, before his death in 2003 he acted as co-owner with his wife. She accepted the NFC Championship medal on January 21, 2007, which bears the name of her father. McCaskey is one of a couple of female

NFL managers, including Martha Firestone Ford (Detroit Lions), Amy Adams Strunk (Tennessee Titans), Kim Pegula (Buffalo Bills), Carol Davis (Oakland Raiders), Denise DeBartolo York (San Francisco 49ers), Gayle Benson (New Orleans).

The Bears under McCaskey

Not too much to say here. The Bears of the 1980s were some of the most fearsome of professional franchises ever assembled. Overall since her 36 year ownership the Bears have been one of the worst franchises of all, albeit an NFC Champion during the 2006 season. As is the case with many owners who inherited a team from their family, there appears to not be much drive to change within the organization. Perhaps an unfair take, but an observation nonetheless.

MINNESOTA VIKINGS OWNER ZYGI WILF

Zygmunt "Zygi" Wilf (born April 22, 1950) is an American property developer. He is the chairman of the Minnesota Vikings of the NFL. Wilf was born on April 22, 1950 in Germany. His parents, Joseph (1925-2016) and Elizabeth Wilf (1932-), are Polish Jews and Nazi-occupied Poland Holocaust survivors. In the early 1950s, the Wilf family immigrated from Europe to the United States and settled in Hillside, New Jersey. Joseph and his brother Harry Wilf started buying apartment houses and renting units after a short stint as used vehicle salesmen. The siblings eventually started constructing single-family homes and established Garden Homes. Since their original ventures, a true property developer, his two primary family-run companies, Garden Homes and Garden Commercial Properties, has built some 25,000 homes in 39 countries across the nation, owning and managing 25,000,000 square feet (2,300,000 m2) in retail.

Wilf attended Fairleigh Dickinson University, graduating in 1971 with a Bachelor of Economics degree, and later earning a J.D. Graduated from Manhattan's New York Law School. President Richard Joel provided him with an honorary doctorate from Yeshiva University at the university's 79th beginning in May 2010. Zygi and his brother Mark Wilf are trustees of Yeshiva University. He obtained an honorary degree at the 69th starting ceremony of Fairleigh Dickinson in May 2012.

Wilf entered the family business after working as an attorney and became the head of one of the company's subsidiaries, Garden Commercial Properties. Wilf has developed the firm from four Northern New Jersey shopping centers to over one hundred properties, including several big shops. The Garden businesses also own and handle 90,000 apartment units across the nation in addition to the business properties.

Wilf and five partners bought the Vikings for US$ 600 million from Red McCombs in 2005. International law firm Greenberg Traurig and now Vikings Chief Operating Officer Kevin Warren offered legal advice on the deal. Forbes estimates the 2018 franchise value at US$ 2.4 billion, 8th of the 32 NFL teams or the 33rd of the 50 most valuable sports teams in the world. Their brand new stadium Bank Stadium opened on the former Metrodome site in July 2016.

In August 2017, Wilf, his brother Mark and cousin Leonard became minority owners of the Nashville SC alongside lead investor John Ingram. In August 2013, Wilf and his brother Mark Wilf and cousin were found responsible by a New Jersey tribunal for violating civil government racketeering legislation and maintaining separate accounting books to fleece former company partners of the Nashville SC. The presiding judge noted that Wilf had used organized crime-like tactics to commit fraud against his company partners. In September, the judge awarded $84.5 million in compensatory damages, punitive damages and interest payable by the Wilfs to the two business partners, Ada Reichmann and Josef Halpern. In June 2018, an appeal lowered this quantity to approximately $32 million.

In 2011, Zygi and Audrey Wilf bought an apartment occupying the entire eighteenth floor of New York's 778 Park Avenue for $19 million, down from its initial December 2009 purchase cost of $24.5 million while still residing in their home in Springfield, New Jersey. Wilf is one of three non-US-born NFL owners along with Kim Pegula (Buffalo Bills).

The Vikings Under Wilf

Yeesh. Not exactly a great look with the accounting fraud. Dishonesty aside The Vikings have remained strong contenders and a dangerous team since Wilf took over. Notable moments include the Brett Favre singing and the 2010 team getting all the way to the NFC Championship, as well as the historic 2017 "Hail Mary" play to Stefon Diggs. Underlying all of this is the fact the Vikings have reached a legendary status nearly up there with the Boston Red Sox, Chicago Cubs, and Buffalo Bills as a team notorious for playoff despair. They made four Super Bowls in the 1970s and lost every single one, and have had some serious tragedy along the way, notably the missed field goal game against the Falcons in the 1998 NFC Championship. Odds are they will finally break their "Curse" but they are understandably still quite a long way off in 2019.

DETROIT LIONS OWNER MARTHA FORD

Martha Parke Firestone Ford (born September 16, 1925) is an American businesswoman. She is the principal owner and chairwoman of the Detroit Lions of the National Football League. Ford is also on the board of the Henry Ford Health System.

Born September 16, 1925 in Akron, Ohio, Firestone is the daughter of Harvey S. Firestone, Jr. and Elizabeth Parke Firestone. Her paternal grandparents are Firestone Tire and Rubber Co. founder Harvey Samuel Firestone and his wife Idabelle Smith Firestone. She graduated from Vassar College in 1946. On March 9, 2014, Martha's husband William died at the age of 88. He had been the sole owner of the Lions since he bought out all other owners in 1963 for US$ 4.5 million. On March 10, 2014 it was announced that controlling interest in the Lions would pass to her. She is the majority owner of the team, with each of her four children holding small shares in the team. Ford is one of ten female NFL team owners. The others are Virginia Halas McCaskey (Chicago Bears), Kim Pegula (Buffalo Bills), Carol Davis (Oakland Raiders), Dee Haslam (Cleveland Browns), Amy Adams Strunk (Tennessee Titans), Gayle Benson (New Orleans Saints), Janice McNair (Houston Texans), Denise DeBartolo York

(San Francisco 49ers) and Jody Allen (Seattle Seahawks).

Ford first met her husband, William Clay Ford, a grandson of Henry Ford, at a lunch in New York arranged and attended by both of their mothers, according to the biography The Fords. She then was a Vassar student who had the college nickname "Stoney." He was a naval cadet at St. Mary's U.S. Navy Pre-Flight School. They married on June 21, 1947 at St. Paul's Episcopal Church in Akron, Ohio. By that time both families had acquired considerable wealth, and the match between the grandchildren of two empire-builders was reported by numerous news outlets. The Akron Beacon Journal called the Firestone-Ford nuptials "the biggest society wedding in Akron's history" and "the biggest show Akron has seen in years" in numerous articles chronicling the event. The couple received gifts from F.B.I. Director J. Edgar Hoover, media publisher John S. Knight, and Mina Miller Edison. The couple had four children: Martha Parke Morse (b. 1948), Sheila Firestone Hamp (b. 1951), William Clay Ford, Jr. (b. 1957), and Elizabeth Ford Kontulis (b. 1961). Her son William was as of 2015 the Chairman of the Board of Directors of Ford Motor Company. He had previously been the Chief Executive Officer and Chief Operating Officer of Ford and is the Vice Chairman of the Detroit Lions.

Ford has 14 grandchildren and 2 great-grandchildren. Ford and her immediate family, and several other members of the extended Ford family, have long lived at Grosse Pointe, Michigan. They originally resided in Grosse Pointe Woods after relocating to the Detroit area following their marriage. She has resided in Grosse Pointe Shores since 1960, when she and William had a house built on Lake St. Clair.

The Lions under Ford

There is no sugarcoating it... The Lions are quite possibly the worst franchise in NFL history. No one would rate their progress since 2014 (When Ford took over) as abysmal, but she inherited a team that has not gone as far as the NFC Championship since 1991, and even recently endured a shameful 0-16 season. Again, the theme of nepotism is here, however unfair to hold it against Ford, who does not oversee the day to day football operations.

THE GREEN BAY PACKERS, OWNED BY GREEN BAY PACKERS, INC.

Green Bay Packers, Inc. is the official name of the non-profit company that owns the National Football League (NFL) Green Bay Packers football franchise.

The Packers are the only publicly owned franchise in the NFL. Rather than being the property of an individual, partnership, or corporate entity, they are held as of 2016 by 360,760 stockholders. No one is allowed to hold more than 200,000 shares, which represents approximately four percent of the 5,011,558 shares currently outstanding. It is this broad-based community support and non-profit structure which has kept the team in Green Bay for nearly a century in spite of being the smallest market in all of North American professional sports.

Green Bay is the only team with this public form of ownership structure in the NFL, grandfathered when the NFL's current ownership policy stipulating a maximum of 32 owners per team, with one holding a minimum 30% stake, was established in the 1980s. As a publicly held nonprofit, the Packers are also the only American major-league sports franchise to release its financial balance sheet every year.

Since August 18, 1923, the Packers has been a publicly held, non-profit company. The corporation currently has 360,760 stockholders, who collectively own 5,011,558 shares of stock after the last stock sale of 2011 to 2012. There have been five stock sales, in 1923, 1935, 1950, 1997, and 2011. Shares in 1923 sold for $5 apiece (approximately $72 in 2017 dollars), while in 1997 they were sold at $200 each and in 2011, $250 each. The NFL does not allow corporate ownership of clubs, requiring every club to be wholly owned by either a single owner or a small group of owners, one of whom must hold a one-third stake in the team.

The Packers are granted an exemption to this rule, as they have been a publicly owned corporation since before the rule was in place. The corporation is governed by a seven-member executive committee, elected from among the board of directors. The commission directs corporate management, approves significant capital expenditure, creates board policy, and monitors governance efficiency in managing the corporation's company and affairs. The elected president, presently Mark H. Murphy, represents the corporation at NFL owners' conferences and other league functions. The president is the only officer receiving compensation. The balance of the committee sits gratis.

At the time of his death, Green Bay Press-Gazette publisher Michael Gage was said to be the largest shareholder of the team. Even though it is referred to as "common stock" in corporate offering documents, a share of Packers stock does not share the same rights traditionally associated with common or preferred stock. It does not include equity interest, it does not pay dividends, it can not be traded, and under securities law it does not have security. It also does not confer rights to buy season tickets. Shareholders receive nothing but voting rights, an invitation to the annual meeting of the corporation, and an opportunity to buy exclusive shareholder-only merchandise. Shares can not be resold except for a fraction of the original price back to the team. While fresh shares can be donated as donations, transfers are technically only permitted between instant family members once ownership has been established.

In 1923 first inventory shares were sold to create the club. Each stockholder had to purchase six season tickets. In order to guarantee that there was no economic incentive for shareholders to move the club outside Green Bay, the initial articles of incorporation of the Green Bay Football Corporation specified that, in the case of the franchise being sold, all earnings from the sale would be donated to the American Legion's Sullivan-Wallen Post

In 1935 a second inventory offer was made to raise $15,000 after the receivership of the company. The non-profit Green Bay Football Corporation was then reorganized as the Green Bay Packers, Inc., the present company, with 300 outstanding stock shares.

In 1950 a third offer was made to prevent the team from becoming insolvent or moving out of Green Bay in the face of the All-America Football Conference competition and the departure of founder Curly Lambeau after a 30-year reign. A limit of two hundred shares per stockholder was introduced to guarantee that no person could assume control and the amount of managers increased from fifteen to twenty-five. Approximately half the potential 9,700 new shares were sold, raising over $118,000 on some 4,700 $25 shares.

In addition to being publicly held, the Packers organization also enjoys substantial support directly from its community. In 1956, Green Bay City electors endorsed financing to build a new stadium owned by the municipality. It was called City Stadium, like its predecessor. On September 11, 1965, it was renamed Lambeau Field.

In 1997–98, the then 1,940 shareholders of the club voted to generate one million fresh shares, offering them at the same time in a split of one thousand to one. The net effect was to ensure that existing shareholders retained the vast majority of voting power. An offering of 400,000 shares followed to raise money for Lambeau Field redevelopment. Running for 17 weeks from late 1997 to March 16, 1998, it raised over $24 million through the purchase of 120,010 shares at $200 apiece by 105,989 new shareholders.

In 2011 to raise money for a large $143-million Lambeau Field expansion, which included approximately 6,700 new seats, new high-definition video boards, a new sound system, and two new gates, a fifth stock sale began on December 6, 2011. Demand exceeded expectations, and the original 250,000-share limit was increased by 30,000. By the offering's end on February 29, 2012, over $64 million had been raised through 250,000 buyers purchasing 269,000 shares at $250 apiece. Buyers were from all 50 U.S. states, and for the first time, sales were briefly allowed in Canada, adding around 2,000 shareholders. Approximately 99% of the shares were purchased online. In the summer of 2011, when the team traveled to the White House to celebrate their Super Bowl XLV victory, Charles Woodson presented President Barack Obama, a Chicago Bears fan, with a share of the team stock.

The team created the Green Bay Packers Foundation in December 1986. It assists in a wide variety of activities and programs benefiting education, civic affairs, health services, human services and youth-related programs.

At the team's 1997 annual stockholders meeting, the foundation was designated, in place of a Sullivan-Wallen Post soldiers memorial, as recipient of any residual assets upon the team's sale or dissolution.

The Packers under Green Bay Packers, Inc.

Simply genius. One has to wonder if more teams would be efficient and further their success by operating under the same ownership structure. The Packers haven't been world-beaters in the NFL since the Superbowl era, but always make a splash season after season and present themselves as a hard out in competition. It is a beautiful scheme that saves a beloved team from Corporate interest, and from being moved from an extremely small market in a larger more commercially viable one. Although grandfathered into this winning formula, you still have to give the teams tons of credit for maintaining a system that has rewarded them with success.

NFC SOUTH

NEW ORLEANS SAINTS OWNER GAIL BENSON

Gayle Marie LaJaunie Bird Benson (born 26 January 1947) is an American billionaire, businesswoman, philanthropist and franchise holder of sports.

After her husband Tom Benson's death, Gayle became the main owner of the New Orleans Saints of the National Football League as well as the New Orleans Pelicans of the National Basketball Association. As heir to the Saints and Pelicans, Benson became the first female to be the majority shareholder in the NFL and NBA franchises on 27 December 2014.

Gayle Benson was born in Gayle Marie LaJaunie. She grew up in Algiers, New Orleans; attended the college of St. Joseph, St. Anthony and Holy Name of Mary; and at 19 years of age she graduated from Martin Behrman High School in 1966. Her first wedding was to Nace Anthony Salomone on April 8, 1967, which ended in a divorce on February 11, 1972. Her second wedding was to Thomas "T-Bird" Bird, on February 14, 1977, in South Pass, Plaquemines Parish, Louisiana, which ended in a divorce on June 25, 1987. Gayle first met Tom Benson in St. Louis Cathedral after Gayle took part in a mass in memory of his late wife, Grace Benson. They married in San Antonio on October

29, 2004. When she first met with Tom Benson, she confessed that the only reason she was interested in meeting him was to receive a gift for a church.

In the 1970s, Benson made her living decorating homes, running dental offices, and later would start an interior decorating business. She was frequently sued and was arrested and charged with theft of furniture from a client. The district attorney declined to prosecute. She had both state and federal tax liens against her business for failure to pay taxes. In the first ten years, Gayle and her then-husband Thomas Bird, renovated one hundred properties.

Tom Benson had planned on bequeathing the voting stock shares of the New Orleans Saints and New Orleans Pelicans to his daughter Renee Benson, grandson Ryan Benson LeBlanc, and granddaughter Rita Benson LeBlanc. However, on December 27, 2014, Tom Benson wrote an email to his daughter and two grandchildren stating he wanted "no further contact with any of you." Gayle Benson, at the time his wife of ten years, was named his heir. Benson's daughter and grandchildren filed lawsuits challenging Tom Benson's decision to name Gayle heir. The lawsuit and media portrayed Gayle as a "gold digger." and questioned Tom Benson's mental competency. Tom Benson was determined to be mentally competent and was allowed to change his estate and leave wife ownership of the New Orleans Saints and the New Orleans Pelicans. Benson became the owner of both the Saints and Pelicans following the death of her husband. Benson is one of ten female NFL owners, including Martha Firestone Ford (Detroit Lions), Kim Pegula (Buffalo Bills), Carol Davis (Oakland Raiders), Denise DeBartolo York (San Francisco 49ers), Amy Adams Strunk (Tennessee Titans), Virginia Halas McCaskey (Chicago Bears), Janice McNair (Houston Texans), Jody Allen (Seattle Seahawks), and Dee Haslam (Cleveland Browns).

In 1989, employees of Gayle Bird Interiors, Ltd., filed a lawsuit in Civil District Court, Parish of Orleans, State of Louisiana, for unpaid wages and attorneys fees. The lawsuit was settled out of court and on March 16, 1998, the judge dismissed the case as abandoned, pursuant to Louisiana Code of Civil Procedure 561, for want of prosecution for five years. Rodney Henry, former personal assistant to Tom Benson, filed a lawsuit accusing the New Orleans Saints and Gayle Benson of racism and violations of federal labor laws. The lawsuit claimed that Gayle Benson had treated him with disrespect because of his race. An NFL arbitrator ruled in favor of Henry and against the Saints on the labor complaint, awarding him overtime pay, a contractual payout for his dismissal, and attorney's fees. The arbitrator ruled against Henry on the claims of racism.

In July 2017, it was announced that Tom and Gayle Benson had finalized an agreement to buy a majority share of Dixie Brewing Co. The company's brewery plant had been damaged and closed after Hurricane Katrina. On August 7, 2018, Benson announced, with New Orleans Mayor LaToya Cantrell, that Dixie Brewery will be opening a distribution center at the old MacFrugal's Distribution Center in New Orleans East.

Benson and her family long have been ardent supporters of University of the Incarnate Word in San Antonio. The Gayle and Tom Benson Stadium officially opened on campus September 1, 2008. In January 2012, Benson and her husband were awarded the Pro Ecclesia et Pontifice for their generosity to Catholic Church, the highest papal honor that Catholic lay people can receive. In November 2012 Gayle Benson and her husband, Tom, donated $7.5 million towards the construction of Tulane University's Yulman Stadium. The stadium, which opened in 2014, brought the Green Wave back to campus for the first time since the demolition of Tulane Stadium in 1980. The playing surface is known as Benson Field. For cancer care and research, the Benson family donated $20 million in 2015.

The New Orleans Saints Under Benson

Yikes. As a franchise the Saints are one of the most well run and renowned winners year after year. The picture painted of Benson is not so nice however, as one has to wonder how close to the mark the accusations of "Golddigger" truly are. The stories about Tom Benson disinheriting his family are particularly sad and hard to believe...

TAMPA BAY BUCCANEERS OWNER BRYAN GLAZER

Bryan Glazer (born October 27, 1964) is a member of the Glazer family, which controls the NFL's First Allied Corporation, the Tampa Bay Buccaneers, and has acquired a controlling stake in the Manchester United English Football Club. The family has its headquarters in Florida.

Glazer was born into a Jewish family, the son of Linda and Malcolm Glazer, American entrepreneur and billionaire. Glazer obtained a bachelor's degree from the American University in Washington, D.C. He then graduated from the Whittier Law School in Southern California with a Juris Doctor degree.

Glazer is currently the Tampa Bay Buccaneers Executive Vice President and was appointed to that position in 1995. He was a main player in designing, developing and building the new stadium in Bucs. He also contributed to the re-design of the franchise logo.

Glazer was appointed director of the Zapata Corporation in 1997 and served in that role until he retired in 2009. Glazer is presently a non-executive director of the Manchester United

Board, appointed by his dad, Malcolm Glazer, to replace the resigned members. Together with Andy Anson (Commercial Director of Manchester United) and Jeffrey Ajluni (Marketing and Business Development Director of Tampa Bay Buccaneers), Glazer was a main player in recruiting AIG for the 2006-07 season as the club's new shirt sponsor.

The Buccaneers under Glazer

Not much is known about Glazer, but his family clearly has strong business acumen, and that has to be admired. The Buccaneers are also an admired team in the NFL, despite being one of the worst teams since their Superbowl victory in 2002. All offense and no defense has been the norm for a team that is never short on entertainment but lacking in the win column.

CAROLINA PANTHERS OWNER DAVID TEPPER

David Alan Tepper (born September 11, 1957) is a businessman, hedge fund manager, and philanthropist, and an American billionaire. He is the National Football League Carolina Panthers owner. Tepper is also the founder and chairman of the Miami Beach, Florida-based worldwide hedge fund Appaloosa Management.

He received a bachelor of economics degree from the University of Pittsburgh in 1978, an MBA from the University of Carnegie Mellon in 1982. In 2013, he donated his biggest donation of $67 million to Carnegie Mellon, whose name comes from Tepper School of Business. Institutional Investor's Alpha ranked Tepper's $2.2 billion paycheck as the highest paycheck in the world for a hedge fund manager for the 2012 tax year. He gained the 3rd position on Forbes 'The Highest-Earning Hedge Fund Managers 2018' with an annual income of $1.5 billion. Tepper disclosed plans to ultimately transform this hedge fund into a family office.

He was raised in a Jewish family in the Stanton Heights neighbourhood of the East End of Pittsburgh, Pennsylvania. As a kid he played soccer and memorized the baseball stats on his grandfather's baseball cards— early proof of what he claims to be a photographic memory. He graduated with honours and obtained a Bachelor of Arts degree in Economics. During college, he also started small-scale investment in various markets. His first two investments were Pennsylvania Engineering Co. and Career Academies, given to him by his dad. Both businesses went bankrupt. He joined the finance industry after graduation and worked in the treasury department for Equibank as a loan analyst. Unhappy with this position in 1980, he registered at the business school of Carnegie Mellon University to pursue his MBA, a Master of Science in Industrial Administration (MSIA) at the time.

After completing his MBA in 1982, Tepper took up a position in Republic Steel's treasury department in Ohio. He was then later hired to Keystone Mutual Funds in Boston in 1984 (now part of Evergreen Funds).

In 1985, Goldman Sachs hired Tepper as a loan analyst who formed a high-yield group in New York City. He became its head trader within six months, staying eight years at Goldman. He focused primarily on bankruptcies and unique circumstances.

After the market crash in 1987, he is credited with playing a significant part in Goldman Sachs' survival. He bought underlying bonds in the financial institutions that had been "crippled by the crash", which soared in value once the market picked up again. He assumed he would be made a Goldman partner but he was passed over, partly because his "loud and profane" manner rubbed other more restrained Goldman executives the wrong way.

In December 1992, after being passed over for partner at Goldman Sachs twice in two years, Tepper quit. He began operating from a desk in the offices of mutual-fund manager and Goldman client Michael Price, aggressively trading his personal account in hopes of raising enough money to start his own fund. He created Appaloosa Management in early 1993. In 2001 he generated a 61% return by focusing on distressed bonds, and in the fourth quarter of 2005 he pursued what he saw as better opportunities in Standard & Poor's 500 stocks. Tepper "keeps the market on edge" and makes significant gains year after year by investing in the "diciest of companies," such as MCI and Mirant. Investments in Conseco and Marconi also led to huge hedge fund profits for the company.

In a 2010 speech he recommended several supposedly risky investments, including AIG debt, Bank of America equity, and European banks. Citing experts who predicted hyperinflation or depression and deflation, he argued neither would happen: "The point is, markets adapt, people adapt. Don't listen to all the crap out there." In 2009, Tepper's hedge-fund earned about $7 billion by buying distressed financial stocks in February and March (including Bank of America common stock at $3 per share), and then profiting from their recovery that year. A total of $4 billion of those profits went to Tepper's personal wealth, making him the top-earning hedge fund manager of 2009 according to The New York Times. In June 2011, he was awarded the Institutional Hedge Fund Firm of the Year. In 2013, Forbes ranked him as top hedge-fund earner of 2012, moving him up to the 166th wealthiest person in the world. Forbes listed Tepper as one of the 25 highest-earning hedge fund managers in 2013 and 2016. In January 2018 Tepper praised President Trump's corporate tax cuts, saying that the bull market still had room to grow and denying it was overvalued. "World growth is higher," Tepper said. "There's no inflation. The market coming into this year doesn't look rich, in fact, it looks almost as cheap as coming into last year." Tepper keeps a pair of brass testicles in a prominent spot on his desk, a present from former employees.

He rubs them for luck during the trading day to get a laugh out of colleagues.

On September 25, 2009, Tepper purchased a 5% stake in the National Football League Pittsburgh Steelers. Carolina Panthers Tepper bought the National Football League Carolina Panthers from original owner and founder Jerry Richardson in May 2018, and was forced to sell his Steelers shares. He beat out a rival bidder with more ties to the Carolinas, Ben Navarro, thanks both to speedy NFL vetting (his Steelers part-ownership allowed the league's owners to bypass the process) and his $2.2 billion bid, the highest in NFL history, much more than other investors

The team's lease on Bank of America Stadium expired after the 2018 season. In a statement, Tepper committed to keeping the team in the Carolinas, and he did. Political giving Tepper and his wife contributed $10,400 to the 2013 Jersey City Mayoral Candidate, Steve Fulop. According to the Jersey Journal on October 24, 2012, "David Tepper, the billionaire who supports tenure reform and charter schools, contributed $10,400 to Fulop's council candidates, while Tepper's wife gave the team an additional $10,400. Fulop's former campaign manager Shelley Skinner became the Deputy Director of Tepper's non-profit Better Education for Kids. In 2015, Tepper donated to both Sen. Charles E. Schumer and former House Speaker John Boehner. In 2016 he donated more than $1 million to PACS supporting Jeb Bush and John Kasich. Tepper supported the Jeb Bush 2016 presidential campaign.

According to Forbes, Tepper has a net worth of $11.4 billion as of February 2017. The Bloomberg Billionaires Index ranked him as the wealthiest person in New Jersey. On March 19, 2003, Tepper announced that he would make a single donation of $55 million to Carnegie Mellon University's business school (then called the Graduate School of Industrial Administration

—GSIA). This donation was made after he had been encouraged by Kenneth Dunn, his former professor (who became dean of the school). He accepted the suggestion but made the contribution a "naming gift" and suggested that the school's name be changed to the David A. Tepper School of Business. Further, in November 2013, Carnegie Mellon announced a $67 million gift from Tepper to develop the Tepper Quadrangle on the north campus. The Tepper Quad will include a new Tepper School of Business facility across the street from the Heinz College as well as other university-wide buildings and a welcome center which will serve as a public gateway to the university. This brings Tepper's total gift to Carnegie Mellon to $125 million. Tepper also has made several large gifts to the University of Pittsburgh, including several endowed undergraduate scholarships and support of academic centers and university-run community outreach programs. Tepper and wife Marlene have pledged $3.4 million to Rutgers University -Mason Gross School of the Arts, the alma mater of his wife. In 2006, Tepper donated $1 million to United Jewish Communities of MetroWest New Jersey toward their Israel Emergency Campaign. In March 2012, Tepper and his former colleague, Alan Fournier founded a political action group, Better Education For Kids. "Better Education for Kids is entering the fray as private organizations are poised to play a larger role in education in New Jersey. Christie wants more charter schools, and he is pushing legislation that would allow private firms to take over struggling public schools. "According to NJ Star Ledger on June 24, 2011," The new group initiated a $1 million campaign last week to advertise its mission and ask for donations. Better Education for Kids, unlike traditional non-profits, is a sort of non-profit that is not needed to reveal its donors.

The Panthers Under Tepper

Wow, what a baller. The author finds this owner one of the most interesting because of his intelligence and will to come from a middle-class background and become one of the wealthiest people in the world. He also bought the franchise from another owner who had clearly lost his grip on life, and was forced out for racially insensitive comments. Although he bought the team after the Panther's most recent Super Bowl bid, the Panthers seem to always be in contention in the win column, and with Mr. Tepper's obviously strong business acumen, should remain at the top year after year.

ATLANTA FALCONS OWNER ARTHUR BLANK

Arthur M. Blank (born 27 September 1942) is an American businessman and co-founder of The Home Depot. He currently owns two professional sports teams based in Atlanta, Georgia, the National Football League's Atlanta Falcons and the Major League Soccer's Atlanta United. Blank graduated from Stuyvesant High School in New York City. Blank was hired by Arthur Young and Company after graduating from Babson College in 1963, where he was a senior accountant. He later joined the Daylin Corporation where he rose to become president of the Daylin division of Elliott's Drug Stores / Stripe Discount Stores. Blank moved to another division, Handy Dan Home Improvement Centers, when Daylin decided to sell off that division. Bernard Marcus was Handy Dan's CEO and Blank was Finance Vice President when both were fired as part of an internal power struggle in 1978.

Blank co-founded Home Depot with Marcus in 1978. New York investment banker Ken Langone brought together the initial group of investors and merchandising expert Patrick Farrah to help founders realize their vision for the do-it-your selfer of one-stop shopping. With its warehouse concept, the store revolutionized the home improvement business, resulting in Blank and Marcus becoming billionaires. Before succeeding Marcus as CEO, Blank spent 19 years as president of the company. Blank retired as co-chairman from the company in 2001.

Today, Blank is the chairman of the Atlanta Falcons and Atlanta United parent company AMB Group LLC. He is also president of The Arthur Blank Family Foundation and serves on Emory University's Board of Trustees.

In February 2002, Blank purchased the Atlanta Falcons from owner Taylor Smith, son of team founder Rankin M. Smith. He bought the Arena Football League franchise, the Georgia Force, in September 2004; after spending several years in suburban Gwinnett County, he moved the team to Atlanta City.

Blank was very interested in buying other franchises. He temporarily withdrew from contention in early 2006 as a potential buyer of Major League Baseball's Atlanta Braves. A few months later, Blank re-entered serious talks with Time Warner and a report indicated that a sale was imminent. However, the Braves completed the team's sale to Liberty Media in February 2007. Blank has also founded an expansion of the 2017 Major League Soccer franchise called Atlanta United FC. The club shares Mercedes-Benz Stadium with the Falcons.

Blank has been married three times and divorced twice, with a third divorce pending. He has three children with his first wife, Diana Blank (born 1942): Kenny Blank, Dena Blank Kimball, and Danielle Blank Thomsen; they divorced in 1993. In 1995, he married Stephanie V. Blank (born 1968), a Blowing Rock, North Carolina native and Appalachian State University graduate he met when she worked as a designer at a Home Depot store in Atlanta. They had three children- Joshua Blank, Max Blank, and Kylie Blank-before being divorced. In June 2016, Blank married to Angela Macuga (born 1968), who has three children from a previous marriage. They announced their pending divorce on January 1, 2019. Blank owns Mountain Sky Guest Ranch and West Creek Ranch in Emigrant, Montana as well as several PGA TOUR Superstores. He is a signatory of The Giving Pledge committing himself to providing charitable causes with at least 50% of his wealth.

Blank reported on February 9, 2016 that he had treatable prostate cancer. Then he announced on March 17, 2016 that after treatment he is cancer-free.

The Falcons Under Blank

Yet another owner with an accomplished life story, Blank tragically is best remember being on the sidelines of SuperBowl LI with his ex-wife celebrating the impending Falcons Superbowl victory. However, the New England Patriots ended up staging the most improbable comeback in Superbowl history after being down 28-3 late in the 3rd Quarter, coming back to win the game in the first ever Superbowl overtime. Year after year, the Falcons remain one of the proudest franchises, always competing, and always showing off an enviable offense. However, their lack of postseason prowess, especially never winning the Superbowl, remains.

NFC WEST

SAN FRANCISCO 49ERS OWNER JED YORK

John Edward "Jed" York (born March 9, 1980) is the current CEO of the San Francisco 49ers NFL franchise, an American sports executive. York is the son of Denise DeBartolo York and John York and the nephew of former San Francisco 49ers owner Edward J. DeBartolo Jr.

York attended St. Charles Elementary School and Cardinal Mooney High School. While Jed is the franchise's operating owner, his mother Denise is the main owner, and both of his parents, as co-chairmen, are responsible for providing resources and maintaining their role of interacting with other owners and NFL executives. On 11 October 2010, with the 49ers starting at 0-5, Jed York wrote to Adam Schefter of ESPN that the 49ers would win their division and make the playoffs. This proclamation led ESPN columnist David Fleming to refer to York as "cooky" and "goofy" and to note that York "supports such bold statements with a long list of qualifications beginning with his lifelong love of the 49ers, his prestigious high school baseball career and the fact that his godfather is Eddie DeBartolo." However, the 49ers came within one game of proving York right that season. In 2011, in the National Football Conference, the Niners finished season 13-3 with the 2nd seed. The Niners defeated the New Orleans Saints in the division round. Then the 49ers hosted the game against the New York Giants in the NFC Championship, eventually losing 20-17. The 2011 San Francisco 49ers' success was achieved with much of the same team as of 2010, but largely with the key addition of first-year head coach Jim Harbaugh.

Jed York was replaced as Team President by Gideon Yu in 2012, although he retained the title of CEO. Following a 19-3 loss to the Seattle Seahawks on November 27, 2014, York tweeted "Thank you 49ers for coming out strong tonight. It was not an acceptable performance. I apologize for that." This public statement sparked a media frenzy over the intentions of York behind the Tweet and whether he specifically referred to the future of Coach Jim Harbaugh.

There was a big negative outcry from the media and the 49ers fan base after the decision to fire head coach Jim Harbaugh. Jed York was quoted as saying in a press conference addressing the issue, "It is up to us to make sure we are competing for and winning Super Bowls. That's our sole purpose. We're not raising banners for the division championship, we're not raising banners for the NFC Championship. We're raising banners for Super Bowl. And whenever we don't deliver that, I hope you will hold me accountable and directly responsible for it. And we look forward to getting this thing back on track." Commenting on York's ability to manage the critical relationship between the general manager and the head coach, Michael Rosenberg wrote in Sports Illustrated, "He failed completely." Rosenberg also described York's impact on the 49's broader organization, noting that " York has created a culture that fosters selfishness, weaknesses and paranoia." Columnist Tim Kawakami of San Jose Mercury News noted that "York and [General Manager, Trent] Baalke were the primary sources of off-the-record disclosures undermining the tenure of Harbaugh."

It was reported that York and Harbaugh had a personality clash. An alleged clash between them worsened the animosity between the two midway through the 2014 season when York allegedly walked into a Harbaugh meeting with the players. When Harbaugh noticed that York was entering the meeting, he allegedly told York that the meeting was for "men only." Trent Baalke replaced former head coach Jim Harbaugh with Jim Tomsula, but Jed supported the change by comparing it with the Golden State Warriors firing Mark Jackson and replacing him with Steve Kerr. Jed's Kerr comparison was criticized by San Jose Mercury News columnist Tim Kawakami.

The 49ers under York

Yet another owner chiefly relying on nepotism to get him where he is, York seems to have not eaten the humble pie but pushed the meme of the bratty owner's son. Still a relatively young man, it is clear he has much to learn about how to run the franchise and not step on toes. That being said, the 49ers remain a year in year out competitor in their division after a decade of complete wasteland football.

THE LOS ANGELES RAMS OWNER STAN KROENKE

Stanley Kroenke (b. 29 July 1947) is an American businessman and entrepreneur. He is the owner of Kroenke Sports & Entertainment, which is the holding company of Arsenal, the NFL's Los Angeles Rams, NBA's Denver Nuggets, NHL's Colorado Avalanche, Major League Soccer's Colorado Rapids, National Lacrosse League's Colorado Mammoth, and the Overwatch League's newly formed Los Angeles Gladiators.

His wife, Ann Walton Kroenke, currently owns the Denver Nuggets and Colorado Avalanche franchises to meet NFL ownership restrictions that prevent a team owner from owning teams in other markets. Ann is the daughter of James "Bud" Walton, Walmart's co-founder.

Forbes estimated his Net Worth in 2018 to be US$ 8.5 billion.

Kroenke grew up in Mora, Missouri, an unincorporated community of about two dozen inhabitants, where his father owned the Mora Lumber Company. His first job was to sweep the floor in the lumber yard of his father. He kept the books of the company by the age of 10. In an interview with The Telegraph newspaper in September 2011, Kroenke said he was lucky— both as he grew up and later in life — to be surrounded by family and friends who saw the value of a good education that he said contributed to his success. He played baseball, basketball and ran track at Cole Camp (Missouri) High School. In 1974, Kroenke married Ann Walton, a Walmart heiress.

In 1983, he founded the Kroenke Group, a property development company that built shopping centers and apartment buildings. He has developed many of his plazas near Walmart stores. He is also the chairman of THF Realty, an independent suburban development company. In 1991, he founded this company in St. Louis, Missouri. In 2016, THF's portfolio was valued at over $2 billion, including over 100 projects totalling 20 million square feet, primarily in retail shopping centers.

In 2006, Kroenke acquired a winery in Napa Valley known as Screaming Eagle in partnership with money manager Charles Banks. Banks stated in April 2009 that he no longer had a personal involvement with Screaming Eagle, leaving Kroenke as the sole owner. Kroenke is a major working ranch owner with a total of 848,631 acres. The Land Report magazine ranked him as the ninth largest landowner in the United States in 2015. Among his notable purchases is his acquisition in February 2016 of the famous Waggoner Ranch in Texas, the largest one-fenceline ranch.

In August 2017, he came under fire for launching a new outdoor sports television channel that was unveiled in the United Kingdom and will show regular hunting programmes that includes killing elephants, lions, and other vulnerable African species.

Kroenke Sports & Entertainment was founded in 1999 and owns Pepsi Center in Denver, Home of the Nuggets and Avalanche, as well as Dick's Sporting Goods Park in Commerce City, home of the Rapids. His development company built both sites. In 2004, Kroenke launched his own competitor to FSN Rocky Mountain (now known as AT&T SportsNet Rocky Mountain), Altitude, a new regional sports network that was launched as the official broadcaster for both Kroenke's teams. Kroenke also set up TicketHorse, a ticket company providing all of his teams with in-house sales.

In 2000, Kroenke became full owner of the Denver Nuggets of the National Basketball Association and the Colorado Avalanche of the National Hockey League, buying the teams from the Ascent Entertainment Group of Charlie Lyons.

In 2002, Kroenke partnered with Denver Broncos owner Pat Bowlen and former Bronco quarterback John Elway to become part-owner of the Colorado Crush of the Arena Football League.

In 2004, Kroenke continued to grow his sports empire by purchasing Colorado Mammoth from the National Lacrosse League and Colorado Rapids from Phil Anschutz from the Major League Soccer.

On 13 April 1995, Stan Kroenke helped Georgia Frontiere move the Los Angeles Rams National Football League from Anaheim to St. Louis by purchasing a 30% share of the team. In 2010, Kroenke exercised his right of first refusal to purchase the remaining interest in the Rams from Georgia Frontiere's estate. Kroenke agreed to hand over control of the Denver Nuggets and Colorado Avalanche to his son, Josh, by the end of 2010, in order to obtain approval from NFL owners, and he had to give up his majority stake in both teams in December 2014. The NFL does not allow its owners to have majority control over major league teams in other NFL markets. On October 7, 2015, the NFL approved the transfer of its ownership stake of the Avalanche and Nuggets to his wife, Ann Walton Kroenke.

In April 2010, as he was trying to gain full ownership of the team and used his knowledge of an escape clause in the Rams lease at the Edward Jones Dome. The arbitrators agreed with the Rams, giving the Rams the ability to break their original lease and assume a year-to-year lease agreement. Saying that he was willing to work with Missouri officials and provide the governor with a "complete understanding" of the stadium situation, Stan Kroenke met with Missouri Governor Jay Nixon at Rams Park in Earth City, Missouri on November 30th, 2015.

On January 5, 2015, it was announced that the Kroenke Group was partnering with Stockbridge Capital Group to construct a 70,000-seat NFL stadium and location in Inglewood, California, a suburb of Los Angeles, threatening the future of the Rams in St. Louis. In response, St. Louis countered National Car Rental Field, a proposed open-air stadium on the north bank of the river in downtown St. Louis, hoping the Rams would stay in St. Louis. At the NFL relocation presentation, Kroenke stated that St. Louis is no longer a viable NFL market, and that only two teams are best served. Kroenke also questioned the financial future of the team. NFL commissioner Roger Goodell also stated that St. Louis funding did not meet the NFL criteria. St. Louis officials opposed Kroenke's misrepresentation of the city and argued that St. Louis was misrepresented at the owners ' meetings. The San Diego Chargers announced in 2017 that they would move to Los Angeles for the 2017 season with the intention of playing games in Carson initially, but then moving to Inglewood Stadium with Kroenke's Rams, pending completion. The Raiders then announced that they were moving to Las Vegas, Nevada.

All three teams applied for relocation for the 2016 NFL season to Los Angeles on January 4, 2016. The Rams and Stan Kroenke released their proposal for relocation the following day. Some of the conclusions of the Rams were disputed by St. Louis Francis Slay's Mayor (in a letter to Roger Goodell), the Regional Chamber of St. Louis, and Forbes. However, some say that staying in St. Louis was ultimately a bad deal for the city and the city is better off with them leaving.

On January 12, 2016, the NFL approved the Rams' request to relocate from St. Louis back to LA. Judge Christopher McGraugh decided on the motions in the case.

Kroenke is the largest shareholder of the Arsenal football club association of Premier League. Arsenal already had a technical connection with Kroenke's Colorado Rapids when, in April 2007, Granada Ventures, a subsidiary of ITV plc, sold its 9.9 percent stake in Arsenal Holdings plc to Kroenke's KSE UKinc. Kroenke continued to purchase additional shares in the club, raising its total stake to 12.19 percent. Initially, the board of the club expressed skepticism that an offer would be in its best interest.

By June 2008, the board had prepared to allow Kroenke to take over the club, and on September 19, 2008 it was officially announced that Kroenke had joined the board of directors of the Arsenal. Kroenke had a beneficial interest in, and controlled voting rights, more than 18,594 shares, representing 29.9% of the shares issued. He thus approached the maximum threshold of 29.99 percent, beyond which he would be forced to make an offer for all remaining shares. On April 10, 2011, it was reported that Kroenke was in advanced talks to complete the takeover of Arsenal. It was announced the following day that he increased his shareholding in Arsenal to 62.89 percent by purchasing Danny Fiszman's stakes and purchasing Arsenal's stakes.

In August 2018, he made an offer of around £600m to the second major shareholder Alisher Usmanov to take full control of the club in a deal that would value the Gunners at £1.8bn. Los Angeles Gladiators In late 2017, Kroenke Sports and Entertainment developed a new sports team franchise called the Los Angeles Gladiators in the newly founded Overwatch League.

Kroenke met his future wife, Ann Walton, a Walmart heiress, on a ski trip to Aspen, Colorado. They married in 1974. Already wealthy from real estate, when he and Ann inherited a stake in Wal-Mart Stores Inc. following the death of their father, James "Bud" Walton in 1995, he accumulated significant additional wealth. This stake amounts to $4.8 billion as of September 2015. He is of German descent and was raised Lutheran. Kroenke is a somewhat reclusive man. He is popularly known as "Silent Stan" because he almost never gives the press interviews. He rarely interferes with the daily operations of his teams.

He donated $100,000 to the Hillary Victory Fund during the U.S. presidential campaign in 2016. He then donated $1 million to the inaugural committee of Donald Trump.

The Rams under Kroenke

Seemingly one of the more cold hearted owners, mostly for strippng St. Louis of their beloved Rams, Kroenke is nonetheless one of the most savvy and impressive businessmen out of all 32 owners. The Rams are the toast of the NFL, at the complete pinnacle of their game, and narrowly missed their first Superbowl ring since the 1999 season. Yet another team who felt the wrath of the legendary New England Patriots, the Rams and Kroenke will dust themselves off for the 2019 season and will be one of the top oddson favorites to make it back.

ARIZONA CARDINALS OWNER BILL BIDWELL

An American businessman, William V. Bidwill, Sr. (born July 31, 1931) is the chief owner and chairman of the National Football League (NFL) Arizona Cardinals. He co-owned with his brother Charles Jr. in 1962 for ten seasons and has been the sole owner since 1972.

Born in Chicago, Illinois, Bidwill and his elder brother Charles were adopted by Charles and Violet Bidwill. Bidwill attended Georgetown Preparatory School, then enlisted in the U.S. Navy until 1956. He went to college at Georgetown University, and after his graduation, moved to St. Louis a few months before the Cardinals moved there.

Charles Bidwill purchased the team from Dr. David Jones in 1933, then known as the Chicago Cardinals. After his death in 1947 at the age of 51, his widow authorized Ray Bennigsen, Charles' business partner, to carry on the team management. In 1949, Violet Bidwill married Walter Wolfner, a St. Louis businessman, and later he became managing director.

Violet moved the Cardinals to St. Louis before the season of 1960. Charles Jr. and Bill inherited the team after their mother's death in January 1962, and served as co-owners for ten seasons until Bill purchased it outright in 1972. Only the Chicago Bears and New York Giants were controlled by one family longer than the Cardinals among NFL franchises.

Little success has marked the ownership of Arizona Cardinals under Bidwill. The Cardinals only made the playoffs eight times in his 57 years as at least part-owner (1974, 1975, 1982, 1998, 2008, 2009, 2014, and 2015). Before the 1988 season, after St. Louis refused to build a new stadium to replace Busch Memorial Stadium, he moved the team to Phoenix, Arizona, despite the fact that the local fans supported the team passionately. Bidwill had also made a public commitment to support a future effort to win a St. Louis expansion franchise. Instead, in Jacksonville, Florida, he voted to approve a new franchise. Eventually, however, St. Louis gained a new franchise anyway, when the 1995 Los Angeles Rams relocated and became the St. Louis Rams. The Rams, of course, came back in 2016 to Los Angeles.

Bidwill has had a reputation for running the Cardinals fairly cheaply; for many years, the Cardinals had one of the league's lowest payrolls. The team started spending more money after moving to State Farm Stadium in 2006. Increased revenue paid off in 2008, when the Cardinals won their division for the first time since 1975 (when the team was based in St. Louis), hosted a playoff game for the second time in franchise history (previously coming as a Chicago team in 1947) and advanced to Super Bowl XLIII. In 2009 and 2015, they won two more division titles.

Bidwill has ceded most of the day-to-day control over the Cardinals in recent years to his sons Michael and Bill Jr., respectively, who serve as team president and vice president. Bidwill also has two other sons, Patrick and Tim, and a daughter, Nicole. Bidwill became the longest-tenured owner in the NFL after Ralph Wilson's death in March 2014.

The Cardinals Under Bill Bidwell

As listed above, and to put it bluntly, Bidwell has been consistently one of the worst owners in the league. If you consider that he is by far the most tenured owner, it only magnifies the depth of his failure at the helm of the franchise. Clearly this has been proven by his overall cheapness in running the Franchise. For decades under Bidwell the Cardinals were the doormat of the league, carrying a stench of playoff futility and one of the worst winning percentages of all time.

Since Bidwell finally turned the reins over to more competent people and started to loosen the purse strings, the fate of the Cardinals unsurprisingly changed. As of 2019, they carried to worst record after a disastrous 2018 season but still have much hype and excitement surrounding their future. With new Qb Kyler Murray and a dangerous WR core, the Cardinals are poised for a major bounceback season.

SEATTLE SEAHAWKS RECENTLY PASSED OWNER PAUL ALLEN

Paul Gardner Allen was an American business magnate, investor, researcher, humanitarian and philanthropist (January 21, 1953–October 15, 2018). He co-founded Microsoft in 1975 alongside Bill Gates, which helped spark the microcomputer revolution and later became the largest PC software company in the world. In March 2018, according to Forbes ' annual list of billionaires, Allen was estimated to be the 44th richest person in the world, with an estimated net worth of $21.7 billion, revised to $20.3 billion at the time of his death. He had a portfolio of investments of several billion dollars, including technology and media companies, scientific research, real estate holdings, private spaceflight ventures, and other sector stakes. He owned two professional sports teams: the National Football League's Seattle Seahawks and the National Basketball Association's Portland Trail Blazers and was a member of the Seattle Sounders FC, which joined Major League Soccer in 2009. Allen was the founder of the Allen Institute for Brain Science, and the Institute for Artificial Intelligence.

Allen was born on 21 January 1953 to Kenneth Sam Allen and Edna Faye (born Gardner) Allen in Seattle, Washington. Allen attended Lakeside School, a private school in Seattle, where he had a friendly relationship with Bill Gates (Only two years younger than him), with whom he shared computer enthusiasm. They used Lakeside's Teletype Terminal to develop their programming skills on multiple time-sharing computer systems. They also used the University of Washington's Computer Science Department laboratory to carry out personal research and computer programming; they were banned from the laboratory for misuse of their privileges there on at least one occasion in 1971. According to Allen, in their teenage years he and Bill Gates would go dumpster-diving for computer program code.

After graduating and obtaining a perfect SAT score of 1600, Allen went to Washington State University, where he joined Phi Kappa Theta fraternity. He dropped out after two years to work as a programmer for Honeywell in Boston, near Harvard University where Bill Gates had ended up. Allen later convinced Gates to drop out of Harvard in order to create Microsoft.

Allen and Gates started marketing a BASIC programming language interpreter in Albuquerque, New Mexico. Allen came up with the original name of "Micro-Soft" (a combination of a combination of "microcomputer" and "software"). In 1980, after Microsoft had committed to supplying IBM with a disk operating system (DOS) for the original IBM PC, although they had not yet developed one, Allen led a deal for Microsoft to purchase QDOS (Quick and Dirty Operating System), written by Tim Paterson, who was employed at the time at Seattle Computer Products. This contract with IBM proved the watershed in Microsoft history that led to the wealth and success of Allen and Gates. The relationship between Allen and Gates, the two technology leaders of the company, became less close as they argued about even small things.

After receiving a Hodgkin lymphoma diagnosis, Allen effectively left Microsoft in 1982. Gates reportedly asked Allen then to give him some of his shares in order to compensate for the higher amount of work performed by Gates. According to Allen, since he "did almost everything on BASIC," Gates said that the company should be split 60–40 for him. Allen agreed to this arrangement, which Gates subsequently renegotiated to 64–36. In 1983, Gates tried to buy out Allen at $5 per share, but Allen refused and left the company intact with its shares. This made Allen a billionaire when Microsoft went public. Gates repaired his friendship with Allen, and the two men donated $2.2 million in 1986 to Lakeside. Allen resigned on November 9, 2000 from his position on the board of directors of Microsoft. He remained a senior strategic advisor to the executives of the company. He still held 100 million Microsoft shares in January 2014.

Allen made some incredibly savvy investments throughout his business career. They include the following. Vulcan Capital is an investment arm of Vulcan Inc., based in Allen's home city of Seattle, which has managed his personal fortune. In 2013, Allen opened a new Vulcan Capital office in Palo Alto, California, focusing on making new investments in emerging technology and internet firms. Patents: Allen held 43 patents from the U.S. Patent and Mark Office.

Allen backed A.R.O., the start-up behind the Saga mobile app. He also backed SportStream, a social app for sports fans and a content-management call app.

Allen invested $243 million in 1993 to purchase 80% of Ticketmaster. In 1997, Home Shopping Network acquired 47.5 percent of Allen's stock in exchange for its own stock worth $209 million. Allen purchased a controlling interest in Charter

Communications in 1998. Charter filed for bankruptcy reorganization in 2009, with Allen's loss estimated at $7 billion. Allen retained a small stake after Charter emerged from the reorganization, worth $535 million in 2012. The 2016 acquisition and subsequent merger of Time Warner Cable with Charter's subsidiary, Spectrum, made Charter Communications the second largest cable company in the U.S.

Allen confirmed that he was the sole investor behind Burt Rutan's SpaceShipOne suborbital commercial spacecraft on October 4, 2004. The craft was developed and flown by Mojave Aerospace Ventures, which was a joint venture between Allen and Rutan's aviation company, Scaled Composites. SpaceShipOne climbed to an altitude of 377,591 feet (115,090 m) and was the first privately funded effort to put a civilian in suborbital space successfully. It won the Ansari X Prize competition and won $10 million.

On December 13, 2011, Allen announced the creation of the Mojave Air and Space Port-based Stratolaunch Systems. The Stratolaunch is a proposed orbital launch system consisting of a dual-body 6-engine jet aircraft capable of carrying a rocket to high altitude; the rocket would then separate from its carrier aircraft and fire its own engines to complete its climb into orbit. If successful, this project would be the first fully privately funded space transportation system. Stratolaunch, partnering with Orbital ATK and Scaled Composites, is intended to launch in inclement weather, fly without worrying about the availability of launch pads and operate from various locations. Ultimately, Stratolaunch plans to host six to ten missions a year. Vulcan Aerospace was announced on April 13, 2015. It is the company within Allen's Vulcan Inc. that plans and executes projects to shift the world's conceptualization of space travel by means of cost reduction and on-demand access. On 13 April 2019, the Stratolaunch aircraft made its first flight, reaching

15,000 ft (4,600 m) and 165 kn (305 km / h) in a 2 h 29 min flight. Stratolaunch CEO Jean Floyd offered this comment: "We dedicate this day to the man who inspired us all to strive for ways to empower the world's problem-solvers, Paul Allen. Without a doubt, he would have been exceptionally proud to see his aircraft take flight". As of the end of May 2019, Stratolaunch Systems Corporation is closing operations

The division of Allen's Vulcan Real Estate offers development and portfolio management services and is known for the redevelopment of the South Lake Union neighborhood just north of downtown Seattle. Vulcan has developed 6.3 million square feet (590,000 m2) of new residential, office, retail and biotechnology research space and has a total development capacity of 10,000,000 sq ft (930,0000 sq ft). Vulcan advocated the Seattle Streetcar line known as the South Lake Union Streetcar, which runs from Seattle's Westlake Center to the southern end of Lake Union. In 2012, The Wall Street Journal called Allen's South Lake Union investment "unexpectedly lucrative" and one that led his company to sell a 1,800,000 square-foot (170,000 square-foot) office complex to Amazon.com for $1.16 billion. one of the most expensive office deals ever in Seattle. "It's exceeded my expectations", Allen said of the South Lake Union development.

Allen opened the Hospital Club in London in 2004 as a professional and social hub for people working in the creative arts. A second location is under construction in Los Angeles.

Allen bought the Portland Trail Blazers NBA team for $70 million in 1988 from California real estate developer Larry Weinberg. He was instrumental in the development and financing of the Moda Center (formerly known as the Rose Garden), the arena where the Blazers play. He bought the arena on April 2, 2007 and said it was a major milestone and a positive step for the franchise. The Allen-owned Trail Blazers reached the playoffs 19 times, including the NBA Finals in 1990 and 1992. According to Forbes, the Blazers were valued at $940 million in 2015 and ranked No. 12th out of 30 NBA teams.

In 1996, when former owner Ken Behring threatened to move the Seahawks to Southern California, Allen purchased the Seattle Seahawks NFL team. Herman Sarkowsky, a former Seahawks minority owner, told The Seattle Times about Allen's decision to purchase the team, "I'm not sure anyone else in this community would have done what he did." The Seahawks were valued at $1.33 billion by August 2014 by Forbes, which says the team has "one of the most rabid fan bases in the NFL". Under the helm of Allen, the Seahawks made the Super Bowl three times following NFC Championship victories (2005, 2013, 2014), and won Super Bowl XLVIII.

Allen's Vulcan Sports & Entertainment is part of the ownership team of the Seattle Sounders FC, a Major League Soccer (MLS) franchise that began play in 2009 at CenturyLink Field, a stadium which was also controlled by Allen During its first season, the Sounders sold out every home game, setting a new MLS record for average match attendance.

The owners and executive producers of Vulcan Productions Allen and his sister Jody Allen, a television and film production company headquartered in Seattle within Vulcan Inc's Entertainment division. Their films were recognized in different ways, ranging from a Peabody to Independent Spirit Awards to Grammys and Emmys. Allen's movie, We The Economy, won 12 awards in 2014 alone, including a Webby award for Best Online News & Politics Series. Among many others, his many other films were nominated for the Golden Globes and the Academy Awards . They include Far from Heaven (2002), Hard Candy (2005), Rx for Survival: A Global Health Challenge (2005), Where God Left His Shoes (2006), Judgment Day: Intelligent Design on Trial (2007), This Emotional Life (2010), We The Economy (2014) Racing Extinction (2015) and Oscar-nominated Body Team 12 (2015).

In 2013, Vulcan Productions co-produced the film Girl Rising directed by Richard E. Robbins, which tells the stories of girls from various parts of the world looking for education. Over 205 million households around the world watched Girl Rising during the CNN and CNN International Premiers, and more than 4 million people worked with Girl Rising through websites and social media. Over $2.1 million has been donated through the associated 10x10 program to help girls receive worldwide education. In 2013, Vulcan Productions also signed up as a producing partner for Pandora's Promise, a nuclear power documentary directed by Oscar-nominated director Robert Stone. It was released on June 12, 2013 at select theaters nationwide and on November 7, 2013 at CNN. A variety of college and private screenings as well as panel discussions were held across the country.

Allen's philanthropy gave more than $2 billion to advance science, technology, education, wildlife conservation, the arts, and community services in his lifetime. The Paul G. Allen Family Foundation, which he founded with Jody Allen, was established to administer the arts and community services. The foundation has given over $494 million to over 1,500 nonprofits since its foundation and in 2010, Allen became a signatory of The Giving Pledge, promising to give at least half of his fortune to philanthropic causes. Allen received praise for his philanthropic commitments, including the Andrew Carnegie Medal of Philanthropy.

Allen launched the Allen Institute for Brain Science in September 2003 with a contribution of $100 million to understand how the human brain works. In total, Allen gave the institute $500 million, making it his single largest recipient of philanthropy. Since its launch, a Big Science and Open Science approach has been used by the Allen Institute for Brain Science to address projects. The institute makes research tools available to the scientific community using an open data model. The Allen Mouse Brain Atlas, Allen Human Brain Atlas and the Allen Mouse Brain Connectivity Atlas are some of the most noteworthy projects of the institute. The Allen Institute is also helping to advance and shape the BRAIN initiative of the White House and the Human Brain Project.

Founded in 2014, the main focus of the Allen Institute for Artificial Intelligence (AI2) is on artificial intelligence research and engineering. The Institute is based on the model of the Allen Institute for Brain Science and is led by Dr. Oren Etzioni, researcher and professor. Four major projects were undertaken by AI2, Aristo, Semantic Scholar, Euclid and Plato. Project Aristo is working to build an AI system capable of passing an 8th grade science exam. Allen committed $100 million to establish the Allen Institute for Cell Science in Seattle in December 2014. The Institute is investigating and creating a virtual model of cells in the hope of delivering treatment for various diseases. Like the institutes before it, all data generated and developed tools will be made publicly available online.

The Paul G. Allen Frontiers Group, which was launched in 2016 with a $100 million commitment, aims to discover and support ideas at the bioscience frontier. In order to survey African savannah elephants, the Great Elephant Census team flew over 20 countries. The results of the survey were published in 2015 and showed rapidly accelerating decline rates. In 2014, he began supporting the Sea Around Us Project at the University of British Columbia to improve data on global fisheries as a means of combating illegal fishing. Part of its $2.6 million funding went to FishBase, an online database on adult finfish. Allen funded the Global FinPrint initiative, launched in July 2015, a three-year survey of coral reef sharks and rays. The survey is the largest of its kind and intended to provide data to assist conservation programs. Allen supported Washington State Initiative 1401 to ban the purchase, sale and distribution of products made from 10 endangered species including elephants, rhinos, lions, tigers, leopards, cheetahs, marine tortoises, pangolins, sharks and rays. The initiative gained enough signatures to be on the state ballot on November 3, 2015 and passed.

Allen and Vulcan Inc. launched the Smart City Challenge alongside the U.S. Department of Transportation (USDOT), a contest inviting American cities to transform their transport systems. Established in 2015 with a USDOT commitment of $40 million as well as $10 million from Allen's Vulcan Inc., the challenge aims to create a first-of-its-kind modern city that will demonstrate how cities can improve the quality of life while reducing greenhouse gas emissions. The winning city was Columbus, Ohio.

As a founding member of the International SeaKeepers Society, Allen hosted his own oceanographic and atmospheric monitoring system SeaKeeper 1000TM on all three of his megayachts. Allen funded the construction of microgrids, which are small-scale power grids that can operate independently, in Kenya to help promote reusable energy and empower their businesses and residents.

Allen pledged at least $100 million in 2014 to fight to end the West African Ebola virus epidemic making him the largest private donor in the Ebola crisis. He also created a website called TackleEbola.org as a means of raising awareness and serving as a way for donors to fund projects in need. The site also highlighted organizations working to stop Ebola that Allen supported at the Ebola Innovation Summit in San Francisco, such as the International Red Cross and Red Crescent Movement, Médecins Sans Frontières, Partners in Health, UNICEF and the World Food Program USA. The summit aimed at sharing key lessons and reinforcing the need for continued action and support to bring down to zero the number of Ebola cases achieved in January 2016. The Paul G. Allen Family Foundation announced in October 2015 that it would award seven new grants totalling $11 million to prevent future widespread virus outbreaks.

In 2012, Allen, along with his research team and the Royal Navy, tried to recover the bell from HMS Hood, which sank during World War II in the Denmark Strait, but failed due to poor weather. On August 7, 2015, they tried again and recovered the bell in very good condition. It was restored and displayed in May 2016 at the Royal Navy National Museum, Portsmouth, in memory of the 1,415 crew members lost. Since 2015, Allen has funded the research vessel RV Petrel and purchased the vessel in 2016. The project team on board Petrel was responsible for locating the 2015 Japanese battleship Musashi. Petrel found USS Indianapolis, USS Ward, the wreck of the Battle of Surigao Strait and the Battle of Ormoc Bay in 2017 at the direction of Allen. In 2018, Petrel found a lost US Navy C-2A Greyhound aircraft off the coast of the Solomon Islands in the Philippine Sea, USS Lexington in the Coral Sea, and USS Juneau.

Allen has set up several non-profit community institutions featuring his historic artifacts private collections. These include: Museum of Pop Culture, or MoPOP, is a non-profit museum dedicated to contemporary popular culture within a Seattle Center building designed by Frank Gehry, established in 2000. Flying Heritage Collection, which displays restored vintage military aircraft and armaments primarily from the World War II era, established in 2004. In 2013, Allen sold Barnett Newman's Onement VI (1953) for $43.8 million at Sotheby's in New York, which at the time was the record price paid by the abstract artist for a work. In 2015, Allen founded the Seattle Art Fair, a four-day event with 60-plus galleries from around the world including Gagosian Gallery, David Zwirner, and many others. The event drew thousands and inspired other satellite fairs throughout the city. Allen announced the launch of the Upstream Music Fest + Summit in August 2016, an annual festival fashioned by Southwest after South. Held on Pioneer Square, the first festival took place in May 2017.

While Allen expressed interest in romantic love and one day had a family, he never married and had no children. His marriage plans were cancelled with his first girlfriend Rita, feeling that he was "not ready to marry at the age of 23." Sometimes he was considered reclusive.

At the age of sixteen, Allen received his first electric guitar and was inspired to play it by listening to Jimi Hendrix. In 2000, Allen played rhythm guitar on the independently produced album Grown Men. In 2013, he had a major label release on Sony's Legacy Recordings; Everywhere at Once by Paul Allen and the Underthinkers. PopMatters.com described Everywhere at Once as 'quality recordings.' Jones said he had extreme respect for Eric Clapton, his band Cream, and Allen in this interview. Referring to Allen's Hendrix-like play, the article referred to a jam session on a yacht with Stevie Wonder.

Allen's 414-foot (126 m) yacht, Octopus, was launched in 2003. As of 2013, it was 14th on the length list of motor yachts. The yacht is equipped with two helicopters, a submarine, an ROV, a swimming pool, a music studio and a basketball court. Octopus is a member of AMVER, a voluntary group ship reporting system used by authorities worldwide to provide assistance to those in distress at sea. The ship is also known for its annual celebrity-studded parties hosted by Allen at the Cannes Film Festival. These performances included musicians like Usher and David A. Stewart. Octopus was also used in the search for a missing American pilot and two officers whose plane disappeared off Palau and among many others the study of a rare fish called a coelacanth. Allen also owned Tatoosh, one of the 100 largest yachts in the world. It was reported in January 2016 that Tatoosh allegedly damaged coral on the Cayman Islands. In April 2016, the Department of Environment (DoE) and Allen's Vulcan Inc. successfully completed a restoration plan to help speed recovery and protect the future of coral in this area

Allen was diagnosed with Stage 1-A Hodgkin's lymphoma in 1982. Although several months of radiation therapy successfully treated his cancer, Allen was diagnosed with non-Hodgkin lymphoma in 2009. Similarly, the cancer was successfully treated until it returned in 2018, which ultimately caused its death by septic shock on 15 October 2018. He was 65 years old. After his death, Allen's sister, Jody Allen, was appointed executor and trustee of the entire estate of Paul Allen, and effectively the new Owner of the Seattle Seahawks in accordance with his instructions.

The Seahawks Under Paul Allen

Like many of his other brilliant accomplishments, Allen's relatively short stint as the Seahawks owner was a resounding success. His fingerprint of success remains on the team even today, as they are still a dangerous and well run team. During the time he owned them the Seahawks won a Superbowl, and for a short stretch were quite likely the most terrifying team to play against in NFL History.

Paul Allen had a simply astounding life, from creating life changing technologies to amassing a stunning personal fortune. He used the money he earned for the good and betterment of the world. Seemingly a genius, Paul Allen excelled in so many key facets of life, from his smart business investments, to his philanthropy, to even being a great musician. His life is truly enviable and it is sad that it has ended so soon. Of all the owners, this author finds Allen to be the most inspiring for his contributions to the world.

About The Author

Bishop Weaver is a lover of history and regularly reads in depth biographies on notable people throughout time. He lives in the Northeast with his Wife and Daughter. Thanks so much for reading!

Can I Ask A Favor?
If you enjoyed this book, found it useful or otherwise then I'd really appreciate it if you would post a short review on Amazon. I do read all the reviews personally so that I can continually write what people are wanting.
THANKS AGAIN!!!

Printed in Great Britain
by Amazon